D0210523

Rekindling Desire

Bringing Your Sexual Relationship Back to Life

by Warwick Williams

B.Sc. (Med.), M.B., B.S.,
D.A., F.R.A.N.Z.P.
Consultant Psychiatrist and
Sex Therapist

5674 Shattuck Avenue
Oakland, CA 94609

Printed in the United States of America

Included with permission are excerpts from
Modern Medicine of Australia, Volume 27, Number 7,
and *The Journal of General Practice,* Volume 1, Number 7

(Originally published in 1986, in Australia, as
Man, Woman and Sexual Desire by
Williams & Wilkins, ADIS Pty. Limited,
404 Sydney Road, Balgowlah, NSW 2093, Australia)

Contents

Foreword

Lack of sexual desire and interest is one of the most difficult sexual problems to treat. However, in recent years strategies have been developed which have made some considerable impact on the problem. Warwick Williams has been one of the leaders in understanding and treating lack of sexual desire. His experience in helping people with this complex sexual problem has induced him to write this book. I have no doubt that it will be of great help to those who read it. It is practical and helps people with this sexual problem to help themselves. When so many doctors hide behind a barrier of impenetrable jargon, it is a delight to know that Warwick Williams has escaped and has written a book in clear English.

Last year I had the pleasure to write a foreword for the first of Warwick Williams' books *It's Up to You—Self-help for Men With Erection Problems*. It is a pleasure to write this foreword because Warwick Williams has done it again!

I recommend that people with the problems of a lack of sexual desire read this book and follow the self-help program so well described.

Derek Llewellyn-Jones

Preface

The material in this book is the result of many years' experience in working with men and women with sexual problems.

It is directed primarily at individuals with deficient or incompatible sexual interests, and their partners, if any, aiming to give them real hope, a working understanding of the relevant issues, and, most importantly, step-by-step detailed instructions for overcoming their difficulties. Many of the issues considered, however, have a universal relevance and importance for perfectly normal people.

I hope that those in the various helping professions will also find the suggested treatment approaches useful in their practices, since there is almost nothing available giving explicit, detailed therapeutic instructions and providing a programmed sequential treatment approach for problems of sexual interest.

I would like to thank all those who have helped and inspired me, particularly Dr. John Ellard, who has guided and moulded my psychological thinking; Dr. Jules Black for constructively reviewing the manuscript; Professor Derek Llewellyn-Jones for writing the foreword; Pamela Petty from Williams & Wilkins, ADIS, for much encouragement and invaluable editorial advice and assistance; Penny Zylstra for doing the illustrations; and last but not least my wife, Elizabeth, who made many suggestions, reviewed the manuscript, did all the typing, and uncomplainingly made available the time I needed to convert my ideas and experience into print. Of course, everything really important that I know has ultimately been learned from my patients, to whom I am deeply indebted.

Thanks are due to the publishers of *Modern Medicine of Australia* and *The Journal of General Practice,* for permission to include portions of articles I have published in their journals.

Warwick Williams

PART I

Understanding Desire

Chapter 1

What This Book Is All About

Whether we like it or not, we are *all* endowed by nature with a sexual drive, interest, urge, appetite, instinct, or libido, to use some of the more common terms. This underpins our actual sexual behavior. The exact nature of this important aspect of ourselves is complex and rather poorly understood, even by scientists. Naturally enough, therefore, there is much confusion about this subject in the minds of many people, and the myths and misconceptions are widespread. One goal of this book is to provide everyone with a practical, working understanding of this part of their nature, and to lay to rest the associated mythology.

Much personal misery and many relationship problems result from misconceptions about sexual drive or interest and its normal variations and fluctuations under different circumstances. For example, many unhappy individuals erroneously believe there is something seriously wrong with them or their partner, simply because they do not understand what is normal. I hope that the information in this book will greatly reduce this avoidable misery and conflict, or better still, prevent it from developing.

Some people are possessed of such a high sexual drive that it causes major problems for themselves or their partners. The book offers such persons and their partners understanding of the main relevant issues and practical guidance.

A very high proportion of the population, at some time in their life, find that they have a reduced sexual drive or interest. Sometimes it may even appear to be absent. This problem may be transient, protracted, or even permanent. In the past, judgmental and derogatory labels, particularly "frigidity," were often applied to such persons, undermining their self-esteem and adding to their misery. Much of this book is devoted to the understanding of deficient sexual drive or interest and to practical do-it-yourself strategies for overcoming it.

Sometimes deficient sexual interest is associated with negative emotions about sexual expression and touching such as anxiety, guilt, anger, or disgust. This often results in an aversion to sexual contact. Much can be done to overcome such aversions, using the self-help procedures described later in this book.

A very common problem in relationships is the presence of significantly different sexual interests in the two partners. While often there is no fundamental abnormality present, this situation has a high potential for causing unhappiness, relationship problems, and even frank sexual dysfunctions. I hope to have provided in this book practical information for preventing such complications of a perfectly normal situation.

Many people feel unnecessarily guilty and/or threatened by what amount to non-monogamous sexual desires. For them, I hope to offer understanding and practical advice, which should overcome these destructive complications of the widespread mythology about sexual desire.

In short, this book is about the nature of our normal sexual drive or interest, and the various problems and abnormalities related to it which can develop. Above all, it is a practical do-it-yourself guide to overcoming associated problems.

Chapter 2

How To Get the Maximum Possible Benefit From This Book

Lengthy experience in working with many clients has taught me that the best results are achieved by following certain guidelines, or principles.

Could I suggest that you will get the maximum benefit if you adhere as closely as possible to the suggestions which follow?

1. Start at the very beginning. *Do not skip any chapters.* You must understand the relevant issues before you can benefit from the do-it-yourself exercises. The early sections briefly cover the minimum basic knowledge you simply must have if you are to be assisted by the exercises. So resist the temptation simply to skim through them. The book is so arranged, that to get the full benefit from any chapter, you must have read and thoroughly understood all the chapters before it.
2. When you come to an exercise in a chapter, do it before you read any further! Do not bypass these exercises and try to read the whole book first. These exercises are absolutely essential for success, and you will get very little indeed from merely reading the text.
3. Make haste slowly. Do not rush through the book and the exercises. Remember, you are playing for high stakes—your future sexual happiness! No matter how much spare time you have to read and practice the exercises, you must realize that it will probably take at least several months to overcome any problems.

4. Do the exercises exactly as instructed. Resist the temptation to do them your own way. They are based on a great deal of experience working with clients over many years, and there are important reasons for them being done the way they are described.
5. If you have a partner, discuss with him or her, on a chapter-by-chapter basis, those issues which apply to you.
6. Do the exercises under good conditions. Do *not* attempt them if you are tired, preoccupied with problems, or feeling upset or unwell. To get the maximum benefit, you must be able to concentrate and apply all your resources to what you are doing.
7. The best way to read the book and perform the exercises is to do a little frequently—perhaps a half hour to one hour most days. This is far more effective than infrequent but lengthy periods of reading or doing the exercises.
8. In a notebook, keep a detailed written record of what you actually do from this book, on a day-to-day basis. This will act as a constant reminder of what has to be done and of your progress.

Good luck!

Chapter 3

What You Need To Know About the Nature and Functioning of Your Sexual Drive or Interest

All of us can easily recognize the experience of pain or anxiety or anger, but it is very difficult for us clearly to describe exactly what we mean, or are experiencing, when we say we are in pain, or are anxious or angry. If you find this difficult to believe, try writing down a definition of pain or anxiety or anger that gives a clear description of the phenomenon and distinguishes it from all other states of discomfort or displeasure.

Likewise, most men and women can recognize sexual desire or sexual appetite and know what it is like, but cannot clearly describe exactly what they experience. In other words, sexual desire is a human phenomenon, usually easily recognized but difficult or impossible to accurately define or even describe.

In medical and psychological circles, one sees the terms sexual drive, sexual desire, sexual interest, libido, sexual instinct, and sexual appetite used to label this sexual phenomenon. In common use to describe this experience is the term "horny."

Sexual Desire or Sexual Excitement?

Although these terms are commonly used synonymously, they really refer to separate experiences. Excitement or arousal usually refers to the state associated with the bodily changes of sexual activation, such as vaginal lubrication in the female and penile erection in the male. Sexual desire can occur without sexual excitement, but obviously can lead to sexual excitement. Sexual desire is, however, not a necessary prerequisite for sexual excitement. For example, generally an individual with no conscious awareness of any sexual drive or interest can be physically sexually aroused, and thus sexually excited, when a partner fondles his or her genitals.

What Is the Nature of Sexual Drive or Libido?

Scientific understanding of this almost universal experience is far from complete, in the same way that much remains uncertain about the mechanisms underlying anxiety, pain, thirst, and hunger. It seems that our sexual drive is generated in our brain, and that it can occur without requiring any stimulus from outside our body. It is also clear that our sexual drive is capable of being profoundly affected by our emotional state, our thoughts, our physical state, and by many influences external to our body.

Sexual drive or libido is experienced as a specific feeling which can cause an individual to seek out, or become receptive to, sexual experience. He or she may be aware of genital sensations, or may feel vaguely sexy, interested in sex, or perhaps just restless.

At a practical descriptive level, it is convenient to regard one's sexual drive as having both a biological and a psychological component.

The Biological Component of Sexual Desire

Without a sexual drive there would be no motive to have intercourse, and the human species would not have survived. Obviously, nature has programmed into us some biological process leading to the subjective experience of sexual drive. This biological drive is perhaps most clearly recognized in adolescence. Teenagers, both male and female, periodically and often frequently, become aware of genital sensations, which often make it hard to concentrate on anything else. These sensations seem to come from nowhere and necessitate some action—either a deliberate effort to put them to one side, or some form of sexual activity, be it masturbation or sexual expression with a partner.

Physiological Mechanisms of Sexual Desire

The most important part of the brain from which, in some unknown way, sexual drive is stimulated is a group of structures technically referred to as the limbic system, located in the "limbus," or rim of the brain. This system is "primitive," in the sense that it appeared early in the process of development which resulted in the complex brain of modern man. In both sexes the sexual function of this system is much influenced by male hormone, or testosterone.

The limbic system of the brain contains centers that enhance or stimulate sexual drive, and other centers which when activated inhibit it. In this regard sexual drive is regulated like other biological drives such as thirst and hunger. When we experience sexual drive, the activating centers have been stimulated and/or the inhibitory mechanisms have been suppressed. When we have no sexual interest, the activating centers have been suppressed, and/or the inhibitory centers have been stimulated.

What Role Do Hormones Have?

Hormones are essential chemicals produced in a variety of glands located throughout the body. They are secreted into the bloodstream and have important effects on parts of the body away from the organ that produced them. A proper balance of all the various hormones is necessary for normal, healthy bodily functioning.

The main hormone regulating biological sexual drive is testosterone, or male hormone. This is produced in two glands—the gonads (testicles or ovaries) and the adrenal glands. The adrenal glands are located on top of the kidneys and produce a variety of very important hormones, not just testosterone. It is important to realize that *both men and women produce testosterone,* although men produce more.

In the absence of testosterone, there is little or no sexual desire. This is clearly seen in clinical situations where the glands producing testosterone are severely damaged, destroyed, or removed. Testosterone replacement therapy in such cases may restore a person's biological sexual drive.

Female sex hormone (oestrogen), which is also present in both males and females, does not appear to have a significant direct effect on biological sexual drive in humans under normal circumstances.

Since normal amounts of all the body hormones are necessary for health, abnormalities of other hormones can affect one's biological sexual drive by indirect, nonspecific mechanisms.

The Psychological Component of Sexual Desire

This operates through other parts of the brain which are interconnected with the limbic system in very complex ways.

While the biological and psychological components of sexual desire are separated for convenience, to facilitate understanding and describing what in reality is a most complex process, it is important to realize that this separation is artificial and arbitrary, and that both components are powerfully interrelated.

At a practical level, the psychological component of sexual desire boils down to a psychological motivation or willingness to have sex. Psychological motivation or willingness is of great complexity, because past and present experiences have a profound effect upon it. Unfavorable past or present events tend to block or reduce willingness, even in the presence of a strong biological drive. Similarly, favorable past and present experiences tend to facilitate and promote willingness to have sex.

Willingness to express oneself sexually can result from a number of trigger stimuli. First and most obviously, an awareness of one's biological sexual drive can activate it. Second, one may make a deliberate conscious decision to become involved in some form of sexual behavior. Third, willingness may be triggered by contact with another person, which could be verbal, nonverbal, or physical, alone or in combination. Fourth, willingness may be activated by hearing of, reading about, or seeing the sexual excitement of others, for example, in movies or magazines.

It is important to understand that psychological motivation for sexual expression, or a willingness to express oneself sexually, is not necessarily the same as a wish to have sex. For example, in clinical practice, I commonly see patients who have no awareness of any biological sexual drive, who are unwilling to have sex, but who wish to be able to have sex with a partner for various reasons. For instance, they may wish to enjoy sex because they feel there is something wrong with them, or because they want to hold onto their partner, and so on. On the contrary, one often sees situations in which a person is aware of a biological sexual drive and a psychological motivation to have sexual contact, but does not wish to have sex. This might be, for example, due to guilt, or a fear that giving in to the sexual drive will have adverse consequences such as venereal disease, pregnancy, or the breakup of one's marriage. In other words, we all have the mental capacity to choose to override the influences of both our biological sexual drive and even strong psychological motivations to express ourselves sexually. Note, however, an equally important point: Just as we can use our mental capacity to override positive libido-promoting influences, so too can we harness our mental capacity to override negative, libido-inhibiting influences. We actually have a much greater ability consciously and deliberately to influence our sexual drive for the better than most people imagine!

The Role of Sexual Fantasy

What is a Sexual Fantasy?

Just a series of thoughts about something sexual which is not actually happening at this moment.

The subject may be completely hypothetical or imaginary, an actual past experience, something engaging our attention at this moment, or some realistic possibility for the future.

A sexual fantasy can be thought of as a day-dream about one of these subjects. Unlike a night dream, however, it is something which can be started or stopped at will, may be very brief, and where we have *complete control* over the script, i.e., over what actually happens.

Some people, but certainly not all, associate these thoughts with pictures in their mind; they see it happening in their mind's eye.

Misconceptions about fantasy are common. Many people erroneously believe

a. It must be about some totally imaginary or make-believe subject or it is not a fantasy.

b. It must be a fairly elaborate, drawn out imagining, like a story. It can actually be almost momentary.

c. It must be associated with mental pictures or it is not a fantasy.

How Does Fantasy Operate?

A simple analogy is often helpful here. Ponder this question: What makes you hungry? Sometimes it is a feeling that comes from within you, unrelated to anything you can put your finger on. Often you will start to feel hungry if you deliberately think about eating, recall a much enjoyed past meal, or look at tempting food, which triggers thoughts about eating.

What you are actually doing in all these situations is fantasizing about food and eating. These fantasies are what made you hungry!

Of course, fantasizing about eating doesn't necessarily cause you to eat. Often when you feel hungry because you have fantasized about eating, you will do absolutely nothing about it, or you will delay eating for some time.

In the same way as hunger, sexual drive or interest can arise purely from within, or it can be stimulated by thoughts (i.e., fantasies) about sex. Our psychological motivation for sexual expression probably operates at least ultimately via sexually pleasing thoughts, with or without mental images; in other words, via sexual fantasies! Some such fantasies of course will be transitory and perhaps barely consciously appreciated.

Note: Sexual fantasies may also be what activates the body systems which lead to sexual excitement or arousal, i.e., penile erection, vaginal lubrication, and so on.

The Inevitability of Sexual Fantasy

Many people when asked if they have ever had sexual fantasies have initially denied doing so, until the simple issues discussed above were explained to them. In point of fact, *we all have sexual fantasies from time to time,* even though the thoughts making them up may not be consciously recognized as a fantasy. Some sexual fantasies (i.e., thoughts about sex) are pleasing, some distressing to certain people in exactly the same way that thoughts about food and eating can be pleasing or distressing.

Note: The intermediary role of sexual thoughts or fantasy is enormously important in the practical management of disorders of sexual desire or interest, as will be seen.

Pseudo-Sexual Interest

Although it may at first seem hard to believe, many people, especially men, think they are interested in sex when they really aren't. This is because they rely on the situation they are in, rather than their own feelings, to define interest. If their situation is one they have learned to label as sexy, such as being with an attractive partner who wants sex, they often assume they are interested, because they feel they should be! Furthermore, as will be discussed in chapter 11, quite frequently sexual behavior is motivated by needs other than sexual interest.

Chapter 4

What Is "Normal" in Relation to Sexual Drive or Interest?

There are many ways of looking at the difficult concept of "normality." Some use a statistical norm; i.e., if most people in a population have a particular characteristic or engage in a specified behavior, then it is statistically normal. In the area of sexual behavior, this is not a very satisfactory approach, because much sexual behavior which is statistically uncommon is clearly not abnormal by any reasonable standards.

Another way of looking at normal is to use it synonymously with "desirable." In other words, behavior or traits that are desirable are normal, and those that are not desirable are abnormal. Since concepts of the desirable vary greatly from time to time and in different societies and are usually ultimately a matter of subjective opinion, this approach to normality is also not very helpful in the area of human sexual functioning.

Another approach is to regard as normal a trait or a behavior that causes no problems for either the individual or the environment in which he operates. This would appear to have a greater applicability in the area of sexual functioning, although it too is clearly not a totally satisfactory concept.

What Is a Normal Strength of Sexual Drive?

Common observation demonstrates that some individuals choose to be frequently involved in sexual expression to relieve a need that is experienced as a sexual drive or tension. Others have a relatively infrequent need for such sexual expression. It is quite impossible logically to say that one or the other is normal or abnormal simply on the basis of frequency, just as one cannot say that a tall person is more normal than a short person.

It is not unlikely that the strength of our innate biological sexual drive is distributed throughout the population in much the same way as characteristics such as height and intelligence. In other words, most of us will be in the mid-range, while a small number will have high and low drives, merely on the basis of population variation. One must remember, of course, that this innate biological sexual drive is heavily influenced in its expression by psychological and environmental factors.

On the basis of all the information available, it can be stated that a healthy young adult who desires and enjoys sexual release two or three times daily is normal, just as is the individual who desires and enjoys such release once every two or three weeks. I would argue that sexual needs outside these ranges cannot be regarded as abnormal, provided they cause no problems for the individual or his or her environment.

Normal Fluctuations in Sexual Drive or Interest

It is a universal observation that one's sexual drive or interest varies enormously, depending on life circumstances. It is normal, for example, for sexual drive to be decreased or absent during periods of pain, stress, fatigue, illness, anxiety, and so on. As will be discussed in chapter 7, one has no right logically to expect to experience sexual drive or interest unless most of one's conditions for achieving this are reasonably met.

It is normal and common for a woman's sexual drive to vary considerably, and often predictably, during her menstrual cycle, although the pattern of this change varies from woman to woman. For example, peak sexual interest may in different women occur during menstruation, just after the period ceases, around the time of ovulation, or in the premenstrual phase. Of course, some perfectly normal women experience no significant change in libido during the various phases of the menstrual cycle.

Many men experience a periodicity to their sexual drive, although this is usually less clear-cut than that often seen in women. Of course, this should not be surprising, since we are all subject to fluctuating biological rhythms or biorhythms.

It is common and not abnormal for a woman's sexual drive to progressively diminish during pregnancy as delivery approaches. Some women, however, find that pregnancy has no effect upon, or even increases, their sexual drive or interest.

Age-related changes in sexual drive are so important that they will be discussed separately in the next chapter.

Is an Absence of Sexual Drive Ever Normal?

The short answer is an unequivocal *yes!* For example, a perfectly normal person whose life circumstances are currently extremely unfavorable may be totally unaware of any sexual drive or interest. An individual who is involved in a committed relationship with a much loved partner may quite normally experience no desire for sexual expression when separated from this partner. A single person without an involved partner may choose to inhibit awareness of his or her sexual drive until a suitable partner arrives. This can be a mature choice, which could hardly be classified as abnormal.

Many people, but certainly not all, feel absolutely no sexual interest toward anyone except the partner with whom they are in love. However, also experiencing a sexual interest toward someone else when one is in love certainly cannot be regarded as abnormal, as will be discussed later under "non-monogamous desires."

It is normal for sexual desire to be inhibited in dangerous or potentially dangerous situations—a moment's reflection will reveal that this is potentially very much in the interests of survival. Of course, there are few absolute truths about human behavior, and some individuals find at least certain dangerous situations a sexual stimulus.

A common situation is seen in a good relationship between a couple where one partner has a substantially higher libido than the other. The less sexually interested partner may then pleasurably participate in lovemaking at a frequency substantially greater than that dictated by his or her own needs. Under these circumstances, the less interested partner may never be aware of any spontaneous libido or sexual need, because his or her sexual appetite is constantly satiated. It is rather like never actually feeling hungry, because one eats more frequently than one's biological needs dictate. Sometimes individuals in this situation worry that there is something wrong with them because they never feel interested in sex, even though they are responsive and satisfied during lovemaking. It can be reassuring to know that this is a normal response to a common situation.

Chapter 5

What You Need To Know About the Effects of Ageing on Sexual Interest

In general, after puberty one's sexual drive increases to a maximum, then gradually declines into advanced old age. The usual time course differs between men and women and there is a great deal of individual variation. Favorable or unfavorable circumstances profoundly influence these normal age-related changes.

Men typically reach their peak of sexual expression (not necessarily synonymous with sexual drive) between mid-adolescence and their mid-20s. Thereafter, the frequency of sexual expression gradually declines. However, in health and in the presence of favorable circumstances, a need for satisfying sexual activity continues into advanced old age.

Women most often reach their peak frequency of sexual expression later—typically somewhere between 30 and 40. Thereafter there is a gradual decline through to advanced old age. The years of the menopause (change of life) may be followed by another increase, for at least a few years, in some women, probably largely for psychological reasons. As with men, in health and in the presence of favorable circumstances, a desire for sexual expression persists into advanced old age.

It is extremely difficult to state what is normal as one ages, as so many other factors adversely influence sexual drive or interest as the years roll by. It may very well be that under truly favorable circumstances age alone has much less impact than is presently thought. It is quite likely that much of any decline in sexuality in later life is due to psychological and socially generated reactions to ageing rather than to the physical process of ageing itself.

An important age-related change for both men and women is that if as they get older they drop regular sexual activity for any length of time, they may have difficulty and need assistance on restarting. One of the most important factors in the maintenance of effective, enjoyable sexuality for ageing people is consistency of active sexual expression. The more you do it, the longer it will last!

Of course, age produces other sexual changes in both men and women. As a broad generalization, all the sexual functions (erections, ejaculation, vaginal lubrication, and orgasm) slow down and require more stimulation to be effected.

A very important age-related change, whether one is talking about libido or sexual organ functioning, is the increasing need to pay attention to one's conditions for being sexually interested and responsive. This crucial concept is discussed fully in chapter 7.

Always remember this: As you get older, there is absolutely no reason (in the absence of major disease) why both a man and a woman cannot continue to enjoy active sexual expression. *The main disability to avoid is the belief that elderly people are or should be asexual.*

Chapter 6

Destructive Sexual Myths

It is almost impossible to grow up in today's society without acquiring and believing quite a number of totally ridiculous misconceptions, false notions, or myths about sex.

How does this happen? Our sexual attitudes are *learned*—they certainly aren't automatic or instinctive! Our sexual learning takes place from a very early age in all sorts of ways, direct and indirect. Information is picked up from our friends, older children (who are just as ignorant), from sexual jokes, glossy magazines, movies, our parents' and other people's behavior), and so on. The early sexual learning we get from our parents is mostly negative, usually consisting of a series of "dont's"! We have very little opportunity of being exposed to and picking up truly accurate information until we are much older, but by then our attitudes to sex and sexual behavior are rigidly fixed, and like all early established beliefs, difficult to change.

We have become surrounded by a system of sexual misconceptions, which is like a prison, within the confining walls of which most of us are doomed to live out our lives. Our sexual behavior has become, and remains, largely controlled by a series of irrational but powerful shoulds, oughts, and musts.

If you wish to maximize your potential for sexual enjoyment and happiness, you must actively break down these restrictive barriers and cease to be unthinkingly and automatically controlled by them.

Let us now consider some of the worst of the numerous destructive sexual myths we have picked up and been hoodwinked into believing, which can adversely affect our sexual drive or interest. Note that the "classification" of these misconceptions is very arbitrary, and there is a great deal of overlap.

Libido Myths

Myth 1. As you get older, you lose interest in sex and can no longer do it. Rubbish! As discussed in the last chapter, you are never too old to be interested in sex! Under favorable circumstances, age has only a relatively modest effect on the strength of your libido. Much is blamed on the effects of increasing age, which is simply untrue, even if it is often convenient. The tragic thing is that if you believe this nonsense, it tends to happen, such is the power over us of our thoughts and expectations.

Myth 2. Too much sex weakens you, and you should ration it. Generations of athletic coaches have probably had a lot to do with the widespread acceptance of this stupid nonsense! True, if you run a competitive marathon immediately after intercourse, you just might turn in a slightly slower time. However, in general, almost the opposite is true. A good, healthy sexual appetite, regularly satisfied, will give you not only more pleasure, but more "get up and go" and enthusiasm in your daily tasks.

Furthermore, if you don't exercise your sexual mechanisms reasonably regularly, you are at risk of losing the ability to be sexually interested and normally responsive. In general, the *more often you exercise them, the longer they will last!*

Myth 3. You can actively force yourself to be interested in sex. With all sexual functions, including the libido one, the harder you try to actively make things happen, in general, the less likely you are to succeed. You can only do whatever is possible to maximize your chances, and then allow your body to do whatever it chooses on this particular occasion.

Superman Myths

Myth 1. A man should not show his feelings. To do so is believed to be emotional, weak, feminine, or even worse, because a "real man" is supposed to control his emotions. The fact that many men manage to do so is a tribute to human ingenuity, because it is certainly a most abnormal state of affairs. This myth possibly causes men more unhappiness than any other single misconception, and certainly has a very destructive effect on many marriages. Furthermore, if you habitually overcontrol your emotions, you are at risk of also overcontrolling your libido and your pleasure in sexual relating.

Even animals are sensible enough to show their feelings! Are you going to go on allowing the average dog to be smarter than you?

Myth 2. A real man is always horny and ready for sex. It sounds ridiculous when you see it written down, and noboby in their right mind would seriously argue in favor of such nonsense. However, large numbers of men act as if they believe it! They expect themselves to be constantly on the lookout for sexual opportunities, act upon them no matter how busy, preoccupied, or tired they are, and be able to respond, perform, and enjoy. The truth is almost the opposite—even the horniest men around only truly feel like sex a small proportion of their waking life, and most find it difficult to respond pleasurably under unfavorable circumstances. Remember, of course, that many men use sex for completely nonsexual purposes and may copulate, not because they feel aroused or sexually interested, but to relieve tension, because they think it is expected of them, to prove their masculinity, and so on.

Myth 3. A real man will automatically know how to make his partner lust after him, and doing so is his responsibility. You may laugh, but many men (and women) act as though they believe this craziness. There is nothing wrong with trying to present yourself to your partner as interestingly as possible, but in no way are you personally responsible for her being interested in sex (or vice versa).

Superwoman Myths

Myth 1. A woman should be sexually interested and available whenever her partner is.

Myth 2. A woman should never be sexually interested when her partner is not.

Myth 3. A woman should always respond sexually enthusiastically and rapidly.

Believe it or not, vast numbers of men and women act as if they expect all this! Looked at dispassionately, it is just insanity.

Myths About Lovemaking (Erotic Follies)

There are so many it is hard to know where to start. Try these:

Myth 1. Lovemaking has to involve sex. For most people, the terms are literally synonymous. Actually, *lovemaking means literally that—interacting physically and emotionally with someone you care about.* Arousal, intercourse, and orgasm or ejaculation are nonessential, and simply possible lovemaking options. I call this the *key sexual attitude.*

This myth is perhaps one of the most important single causes of sexual unhappiness, and overcoming it, by developing the key sexual attitude, is crucially important if you wish to resuscitate your sex life, or maximize your sexual potential. This key attitude will be discussed further in chapter 10 and in session 1.

Myth 2. Pleasurable physical contact must go on to sex. Men have often grown up with the idea that for them only two kinds of body contact are permissible: aggressive and sexual. This means that touching a woman without a view to sex is unacceptable. You may be surprised to know that one of the commonest serious complaints women have about men is that "he only holds, cuddles, or strokes me when he wants sex." Women, quite understandably, feel resentful about this.

We all have an innate need for touching with other humans (Skin Hunger) and there is absolutely nothing wrong with this. By no possible stretch of the imagination is it unmanly. It can be very comforting sometimes simply to be held and stroked.

If you have got into the bad habit of only touching when you want sex, it will take you a while to get out of it, but you will be truly amazed at the difference it makes when you are able to engage in stroking, holding, cuddling, and so on, with no sexual intent. While touching and sex remain linked together in your mind, you can't touch without putting pressure on yourself and your partner to be sexual, when perhaps this is not really desired by either of you.

Myth 3. You can't participate in lovemaking and enjoy it unless you feel horny. This is really a corollary of lovemaking myth 1 and absolutely untrue. It is discussed further in chapter 10.

Myth 4. Sex must lead to orgasm.

Myth 5. Once started, sex must continue until orgasms have been achieved.

Myth 6. A couple should reach orgasm at the same time.

These orgasm myths can be considered together. It is totally inconceivable to many people that anyone could want sex but not wish or need an orgasm. However, this is a commonplace experience, particularly for women, and for men as they get older. It is quite possible and perfectly normal for a person to feel a desire or need for the closeness and other emotional gratifications of sexual contact but not feel like having an orgasm. You both need to know that as men get older, their need for an orgasm to complete a rewarding sexual experience normally decreases. Many older men will tell you that quite often they feel horny and want intercourse but are not really interested in having an orgasm, and there is absolutely nothing wrong with that! If you feel you or your partner simply must wind up having an orgasm whenever you have sex, you are putting pressure on your sexual relationship, which will cause you trouble, sooner or later.

Many men and women erroneously believe that once sexual stimulation begins it must continue uninterruptedly until orgasm is achieved. The notion that during lovemaking one or both partners might like to have a rest, or listen to some music, or even have a sleep, before continuing, is just totally incomprehensible! In actual fact, you will be pleasantly surprised to discover that often the most intense heights of sexual arousal and pleasure are attained by lovemaking that stops and starts, rather than progresses without any pause. Try it yourself, and when it no longer seems odd, you may be in for a real treat.

The absurd and destructive simultaneous orgasm myth dies hard. Even now that most men and women know as an intellectual fact that only a minority of women can achieve orgasm purely from the stimulation of intercourse, they still fuss about climaxing with their partner! It is actually quite an improbable feat for a couple to climax together, and it is usually achieved by one partner desperately trying to hold off orgasm, while the other equally frantically tries to climax sooner. If one or the other fails, there is often disappointment, frustration, a tendency to put oneself down, and the like. Bedroom olympics like this, with a win-or-lose agenda, are a recipe for unhappiness. The really sad fact about this whole pathetic misconception is that truly sharing your partner's orgasm, by being able to observe it and experience it, is extremely emotionally rewarding, but it is impossible if you are coming at the same time. You are too tied up blowing your own mind to enjoy the spectacle of him or her doing the same thing.

Myth 7. Sex must be spontaneous. If you believe this, there is no place for premeditated sex, where you might, for example, have got rid of the kids for the day, moved your stereo into the bedroom so you can play romantic music, chilled a bottle of champagne, and taken your favorite erotica out of their hiding place so you can enjoy them together in bed! While there is absolutely nothing wrong with spontaneous, impulsive sex, such as a quickie in your car before you get home from a dinner party, do not close your mind to the extra joys that can result from planned lovemaking. For some reason, many women are more hung up about this than men.

Myth 8. It's performance that really counts. Many people have been brainwashed into believing that their personal worthwhileness and masculinity or femininity is directly related to how well they perform. *A performance orientation is a real liability in the sexual area,* because if you are thinking about how well or otherwise you are measuring up, you can't tune in to your emotions, your feelings, or your partner, and truly enjoy yourself! Furthermore, if for some reason you judge your performance as not measuring up to your expectations, you will feel anxious, angry, or dejected, and these emotional responses will spoil your pleasure and impair your performance, setting up a vicious cycle.

The truth, or course, is that all that really counts is sharing an enjoyable, unique, physical and emotional closeness with someone you really like or love. Anything more is just an optional extra. I don't expect you to believe this just because I say it, but at least try it for a while, and see whether in fact both you and your partner actually do enjoy your lovemaking much more. See if you don't feel so much better when you don't have to worry about turning in a top-rating performance.

Myth 9. Lovemaking ability comes naturally. This is particularly a misconception of men. I presume that they choose to believe this because sex is indeed a natural body function. A wise Frenchman once said that making love is like playing a delicate violin skillfully and requires about as much intuition and practice. I see no reason to disagree with him in any way. Unfortunately, many men's egos just can't cope with the idea that they might need to learn to be sensual and erotic.

Myth 10. Good sex must be super-sex. If you believe this, you won't enjoy lovemaking unless it turns out to be a five-star extravaganza. You will certainly not enjoy a five-minute quickie without the trimmings when you are horny but running late for work, or going to sleep in each others' arms soon after penetration because you are both dead tired. A sexual blockbuster is great if you have the time and opportunity, but you will be much happier sexually if you lower your goals considerably and learn how to enjoy basic physical and emotional closeness.

Myth 11. Men must always be active during sex and women should be passive.

Myth 12. Men are responsible for what happens during sex.

Myth 13. During sex the male is responsible for his partner's arousal and orgasm.

Myth 14. If he really loved me, he would automatically know what I like and need during sex.

These last four myths can be considered together, as they are closely related. Men and women are of course equal, both generally and sexually, and have the same sexual rights and responsibilities. There is absolutely no rational reason why a man should feel responsible for everything that happens during lovemaking, as if he had to orchestrate the whole performance! What happens is surely a shared responsibility. Just as from time to time a woman will feel like being relatively passive sexually, so sometimes will a man, this being perfectly right and proper. Nonetheless, many men find it very difficult just to lie back and do nothing, passively soaking up the attentions of their partners. Likewise, a lot of women only feel comfortable when they adopt a passive role during lovemaking. Being active is seen as unfeminine.

During lovemaking, each partner is personally responsible for his or her own arousal and orgasm. It is our own responsibility to make sure that we get the kind of stimulation we wish or need, where we want it, for as long as we choose. Our only responsibility to our partner is to do our best to give him or her what seems wanted. This whole issue of responsibility is so crucially important for good lovemaking that it will be considered again in the next chapter.

Marital Myths

Myth 1. Once you are married, life together, and sex in particular, should be bliss. This may have happened in the fairytale stories we listened to as kids, but in the real world marriage is a difficult business, inevitably with pressures, worries, conflicts, and the like. In a good relationship, marital sex varies in quality from time to time from unpleasant to great. If you expect things to be automatically perfect, or even good, you are going to be constantly disappointed and frustrated. You may erroneously think that there is something fundamentally and seriously wrong with your relationship.

Myth 2. There is no such thing as sexual monotony if you truly love your partner. Sadly, even love is not sufficient to keep your sex life exciting and stimulating. It will only remain this way if you keep working at it, using your joint erotic imaginations to the fullest. After the initial excitement and novelty of getting to know each other wears off, many couples find that their lovemaking gradually becomes something of a predictable routine with not much variation. Sexual monotony has set in. Some seek to rekindle sexual excitement with a different partner, others erroneously believe the situation is an inevitable consequence of ageing, often leading them to give up on sex altogether. As the excitement of lovemaking decreases, so does your interest in it.

Myth 3. One partner has the right to make the rules (general and sexual) in this relationship. Even if you both believe in equality and try to practice it, you will find that without thinking about it and certainly without discussing it, one or both of you have laid down ground rules in certain areas of your relationship. In other words, you have certain very definite expectations which have never been mutually agreed upon, and you get annoyed or disappointed when your partner doesn't meet them. He or she may not even know what they are!

Myth 4. My partner should be interested in sex when I am.

Myth 5. In a good marriage, you should never wish or need to masturbate.

Myth 6. When your partner masturbates, that means there is something wrong with you.

These three myths can be conveniently considered together. It is unusual for both partners, even in a very good relationship, to feel like sex at the same time. It is also inevitable from time to time, even in excellent marriages, that one partner feels anti-sex when their mate is horny. The various ways of optimally handling these normal situations are discussed in detail in chapter 10. Solo masturbation can be a perfectly normal, even desirable option under these circumstances. Furthermore, sometimes one may feel a need to relieve sexual tension but have absolutely no interest in, or wish for, partner contact. One might even feel anti-partner contact at this particular moment. Under these circumstances, masturbation is perfectly normal and certainly nothing to feel guilty about.

If you find that your partner has been masturbating, avoid the mistake of instantly personalizing the situation and jumping to the conclusion that it is because he or she doesn't find you attractive, no longer loves you, thinks you are a lousy lover, and so on. Even in the best marriages, both men and women will from time to time simply feel like masturbaing, and this is abolutely normal! Of course, if despite an available caring and willing partner you habitually prefer to masturbate alone instead of making love together, then something has indeed gone wrong!

Myth 7. Children should have no effect on your sex life.

Myth 8. Children's needs should always have priority.

One way or the other, the presence of children and one's responsibilities for them can profoundly, and usually adversely, influence one's sex life. This happens mainly by interference with your "conditions" for being sexually interested and responsive, something which will be discussed in the next chapter.

Many parents, especially mothers, make the mistake of habitually putting the wishes and needs of the children ahead of their own. This is a common cause of personal unhappiness and marital conflict. Remember, you also have a responsibility to your partner, and to yourself. The most happiness for everyone in the family will result when you aim to strike a happy balance between these three responsibilities.

How To Overcome Sexual Myths

This is not easy, but is absolutely essential, and it will take you some considerable time. You certainly won't make any progress at all just by being aware of the stupidity of these myths. The only practical way to change these faulty attitudes is to alter your behavior, to get in there and actively do something relevant. Get stuck into the following exercises before you read on. Get your partner to do them, too.

1. Go through the myths listed in this chapter and *write down* those that you feel have some effect on you.
2. For each myth affecting you, do the following:
   a. Write down all the numerous, practical ways in which this myth has caused problems or difficulties for you. Illustrate each with an actual example from your past.
   b. Write down all the reasons you can think of why the myth and its consequences are ridiculous and destructive. Give this some real thought; take your time.
   c. If at all possible, discuss in detail what you have done in a. and b. with your partner.
3. Rewrite your entire list of personally relevant myths, but now in logical rational terms. For example, if a relevant myth affecting you is this: "During sex the male is responsible for his partner's arousal and orgasm," rewrite it, something like this: "I am not responsible for my partner's arousal and orgasm—she is! My only responsibility to her is to do my best to give her what she lets me know she wants."

4. Read both your own and your partner's lists of logically rewritten myths out loud once a day, with feeling. Continue doing this until you have completely finished working on your libido problem.
5. For each personally relevant myth, work out and write down some actual corrective behaviors, or things to do to help you overcome the destructive effects of the myth. For example, take the myth "pleasurable physical contact must go on to sex." Your corrective behaviors might involve things such as
   a. "I will make a deliberate effort to stroke, cuddle, and touch my partner as often as I can in situations where there is no possibility of sex, such as just before I leave for work, when we go out together, while driving, and so on."
   b. "I will frequently engage in deliberate, gentle sexual touching, such as breast and genital fondling and stroking, but without following through and making love. I will do this sometimes when we watch TV together alone, sometimes when we go to bed, sometimes when we have a brief spontaneous cuddle around the house. Even if I then feel like following through, I will deliberately stop myself."
6. Make a definite ongoing effort to carry out your personal corrective behaviors as often as possible. You will find that it is best to hammer away repeatedly at the corrective behaviors directed at only one myth at a time, rather than several or the whole lot. When you feel you have reasonably changed a particular faulty attitude, then and only then have a crack at your corrective exercises directed at the next myth you wish to tackle.

A Few Important Practical Tips

1. Do these exercises thoroughly—don't rush through them. It will take some considerable time, but it is time very well spent. Remember, your future sexual happiness is at stake.
2. A little done often is better than trying to do everything in one long session.
3. When you have finished each written exercise, put it away for a few days, then go through it again to see if you have any new ideas about it.
4. Don't make the mistake of persuading youself that you will read the whole book first, then come back and do these exercises. To get the maximum benefit, you simply must do the necessary exercises as you come to them!
5. Share as much as possible of what you are doing with your partner. The more he or she is involved and understands, the easier everything will be for you.

6. Whatever else you do, make certain you develop the key sexual attitude, described above. This is so important that I have offered some hints that should help in session 1.
7. Should you realize that you need more powerful guns to bring to bear against a myth you find particularly difficult to overcome, try the additional suggestions in session 4.

Chapter 7

Your Conditions or Requirements for Being Sexually Interested or Responsive

This is one of the most critically important chapters in this book.

Pay great attention to it!

The message of this chapter can be very simply stated: Nobody, male or female, has any rational grounds for expecting to be sexually interested or responsive during sexual activity unless his or her own personal conditions or requirements for being sexually interested and responsive are reasonably met. The older one gets, the more important this becomes.

What Are "Necessary Conditions"?

A condition is essentially anything that can affect your ability to be sexually interested, or to respond sexually. In other words, it is something the presence or absence of which makes it easier for you to be interested or responsive. It may be something in you, in your partner, in your relationship, or in your environment.

What Are Your Necessary Conditions?

As a rule, these are a personal, individual matter, although some are applicable to most people. These general conditions will now be described.

1. Not being too tired. If you are tired, you have no rational grounds for expecting to be sexually interested or responsive. Chronic fatigue in particular is very destructive!

2. Absence of significant physical discomfort. If you have a nasty headache, or your back is playing up and causing a lot of pain, or if you are in any way significantly uncomfortable or feeling unwell, it is ridiculous to expect to be interested in sex or to have your sexual mechanisms function normally.

3. Absence of emotional "uptightness." If you are feeling guilty, frustrated, angry, worried, or miserable and down in the dumps, do not expect to be interested or responsive, since these emotional states can have a very powerful inhibiting effect on your interest and responsiveness.

4. Presence of at least some degree of pleasurable anticipation. If past experience has demonstrated that sexual encounters aren't very rewarding or enjoyable, you are not likely to be busting at the seams to make love.

5. Presence of some attraction to your partner. If you are not interested in or attracted to your partner, why on earth would you wish to make love with him or her? On what vaguely rational grounds can you possibly expect to be sexually interested and responsive under these circumstances?

6. Absence of concern about your own sexual performance. If you are concerned about (or thinking about) how well or otherwise you will perform or about what your partner will think of your lovemaking, you are activating one of the most powerful and destructive inhibitors of interest and responsiveness.

7. Absence of tension in your relationship with your partner. If you are feeling negative toward your partner, your sexual mechanisms will probably react as though they feel exactly the same way. It may in fact take some time after your negative feelings have been overcome before your sexual mechanisms are able to function as you would wish.

For example, you cannot logically expect to be normally interested and responsive five minutes after an argument with your partner has been resolved. This condition tends to be even more important for women.

8. Absence of unhelpful thoughts. Even if you are not emotionally uptight, if some unresolved problem or issue from the day is still ticking in your mind, you may find your libido suppressed and that your sexual apparatus won't function properly.

9. Presence of adequate mental and physical stimulation. Especially as you get a bit older, you cannot expect to be responsive just because you happen to be in a sexual situation with your partner. Particularly if lovemaking has become a fairly stereotyped ritual, no matter how much you love your partner and how attractive you find him or her, you may not find the sexual situation stimulating or arousing enough to generate an adequate physical response.

10. Presence of an adequate physical environment. Are you free from the possibility of interruption? Do other people nearby know what you are doing or can they hear you? Are you expecting the phone to ring at any moment? Are you too cold or too hot? Common sense dictates that lovemaking needs to occur in an adequate environment, without which it is unreasonable and stupid to expect to be interested and responsive.

11. Absence of too much alcohol (or other sedative drugs). Remember, the amount of alcohol in your blood which is required to impair your ability to be interested and responsive varies considerably from person to person. Some are adversely affected by even small amounts. Of course, in some individuals, small amounts of alcohol may appear to increase sexual drive. When this is seen, it is really due to the alcohol reducing their psychological inhibitions. Even in such persons, larger amounts suppress interest and responsiveness.

Male/Female Differences in Conditions

As a broad generalization, young men's sexual nervous systems are sometimes so excitable that their interest and responsiveness seem relatively immune to adverse conditions. Even when this is the case, this situation changes as they get older.

A woman's desire tends to be more affected by love, warmth, intimacy, and meaningful communication than a man's. Oftentimes, unless her emotional needs are met, interest and responsiveness are blocked. Likewise, for a woman, what one might loosely call "the right atmosphere" is often highly important, a fact generations of male seducers have known and exploited.

A woman's desire and responsiveness tends to be even more susceptible to psychological influences, internal and external, than a man's. As the saying goes, "biology moves her, but psychology rules her."

The sex drives of men and women are often affected by different influences. *Sometimes the very thing that turns him on, switches her off!* For example, men in general are often very responsive to visual stimuli such as nakedness, erotic books, magazines, and movies. Many women have no response, or an adverse response to these things. While women often respond to romantic movies and nonsexual closeness and intimacy, many men find these boring or even a turnoff.

There are, of course, numerous exceptions to these generalizations, but the basic message should be clear: there are often significant differences between male and female conditions for being sexually interested and responsive. It behoves all of us to understand not only our own conditions, but also our partner's. Both men and women have a tendency to assume, without checking, that what they like or need, their partner likes or needs! This assumption can cause much misunderstanding and sexual unhappiness.

Some General Issues

Many people, mainly men, that I have counselled have found it hard to accept their need to pay attention to some of these conditions, arguing that previously they have been able to be adequately interested and responsive despite the absence of these requirements. Others cite people known to them who can (or allege they can) be responsive and perform under any circumstances, no matter how adverse. It is true that there are a few people, mainly men, whose libido and responsiveness seem largely unaffected by their emotional or physical state—as if somehow their sexual circuitry was insulated from their feelings. You might envy this ability, but not logically, because more often than not such people pay a terrible price for this ability. They are unable to experience much real pleasure from sexual relating.

We must all understand and accept that getting older produces changes in our pattern of sexual interest and responsiveness, and one crucial change is that we simply have to begin paying attention to our conditions for being interested and responsive. This becomes progressively more important as we get older! The fact that perhaps previously you could ignore many conditions and still be interested and respond, certainly does not mean you can keep on ignoring them. You just have to accept the fact that sooner or later you and every one else are going to be *forced* to pay attention to your conditions whether you like it or not.

Many men who have been reared on a solid diet of sexual myths, from which few of us can escape, feel that having conditions for being interested and responsive is a sign of weakness or inadequacy, unmanly, feminine, and so on. They find the idea of conditions almost repugnant. If this is how you feel, you had better start working on changing these ridiculous attitudes, or in the long run you will pay a terrible price (in unhappiness). I can assure you that you will have much more success changing your irrational beliefs than you will have trying to alter your conditions for being interested and adequately responsive.

How To Work Out Your Conditions

If you have a partner, you should both do these exercises, even if he or she has no obvious sexual problems.

When you have privacy and are not tired or preoccupied, sit down with paper and pen nearby, and with your eyes closed, think of the most recent sexual experience you can remember which you found very satisfying and where you had no problems. Run through the whole encounter in your mind, from the very earliest stages to the end. When you have done this, write down all the factors you can think of that contributed to such a successful outcome—in yourself, your partner, your relationship, and in the general environment. When you have finished as best you can, run through the general conditions discussed in this chapter, and see whether they too applied. If so, add them to your list.

If you have not had an exciting and successful sexual encounter that you can recall, sit back and imagine in detail a make-believe ideal encounter, then work out some of your conditions as above.

Next, run through in your mind the worst, most unsatisfactory sexual encounter you can remember, using this to work out more of your conditions, exactly as described above. When you have finished, run through my list of general conditions and see how they applied to that unsatisfactory encounter. Write down what you have learned.

When you have done both these exercises, see if you can think of anything else at all which does, or could possibly, affect for better or worse the pleasure or satisfaction you would experience in a sexual encounter. Write these down. Remember, a condition is basically absolutely anything that affects your ability to be sexually interested or responsive.

When you have both run out of fresh ideas about your conditions, see if you can discuss everything each of you has written down. Make sure your partner gets you to clarify everything so that he or she knows exactly what you mean. Avoid communicating in generalities—be absolutely specific! For example, saying, " I need to feel loved" is far too general. This needs to be expanded considerably—what exactly must you do or say, or not do or not say, so that you feel your partner loves you?

If you don't have a partner with whom you can discuss these issues, pretend you are your partner, and ask yourself the sort of questions a real partner would ask to clarify precisely what you mean.

When all this has been done, summarize everything you have learned about yourself from this chapter and the exercises. In other words, write down your definitive list of your conditions for being adequately sexually interested and responsive. Make sure they are written in absolutely practical terms, not generalities. Exactly what you need must be crystal clear.

Check that your list contains as a condition something like this: "Knowing and accepting that arousal and performance are not in any way necessary for satisfactory and successful lovemaking." This is absolutely essential.

Keep your final list and your partner's somewhere handy, so that you can read them through carefully aloud and with feeling, once daily, for the remainder of the time you are working on overcoming your libido problem.

With the passage of time, you will probably find that your "final" lists grow as you both become increasingly aware of all the various additional factors which affect your sexual behavior. You will get valuable extra information from the practice of self-monitoring described in session 5.

If you can, explain to as many friends and acquaintances as possible, both male and female, the general issue of conditions for being sexually interested and responsive. Counter any argument, as I have tried to do in this book. By teaching others, you are impressing these very important notions much more firmly in your own mind, and this will help you even more.

Your Sexual Rights and Responsibilities

Men and women are equals, generally and sexually. This means that they have the same sexual rights and responsibilities. An important condition for good lovemaking is that you are able to easily, comfortably, and appropriately exercise your sexual rights and responsibilities.

Contrary to the erroneous views held by many men and women, a man is *not* responsible for his partner's arousal and ultimate orgasm—*these are her responsibilities!* A man's only responsibility to his partner is to do his best to give her the kind of stimulation she desires on any particular occasion. If she doesn't clearly communicate her needs and wishes and therefore misses the boat, that is her problem and her responsibility, not his! Naturally, the same applies in reverse.

Of course, this is not to say that each partner must always do exactly what the other wishes. Some forms of stimulation enjoyed by one may be unacceptable to the other, and there is certainly no law stating that you have to do something you find unacceptable! If there is conflict between you and your partner over performing some kind of sexual behavior, discuss the issues when you are *not* in a sexual situation, and see if you can come to understand each other's point of view, and then perhaps agree to some mutually acceptable compromise.

As an equal partner in a sexual relationship, you have certain rights, which are exactly the same as those of your partner. You have the right to ask for or to initiate lovemaking; he or she of course has the right to decline. You have the right to ask for any particular form of stimulation or activity you desire, including sexual contact without orgasm or without intercourse. You have a right during lovemaking to cease personal participation if you no longer feel like it. Of course, hopefully you would then offer to relieve your partner's sexual tension by manipulating him or her to orgasm, should he or she desire this. You also have a right to express how you feel about any aspect of lovemaking. However, be very gentle if ever you have to say anything even vaguely critical about your partner's lovemaking. All humans are extremely vulnerable to even minor criticism of their sexual prowess. Some hints on improving your sexual communication are offered in session 16.

You might now say that you accept the fact of your rights, but would find it difficult or impossible actually to exercise them with a partner. In other words, you just could not say the appropriate things to him or her, even though you have every right to do so. Apart from working to improve your general sexual communication, a simple way to overcome this difficulty is repeatedly to practice saying the kinds of things you would find difficult to say to him or her into a tape recorder. Listen to the playback and give yourself constructive criticism and appropriate praise. Repeat one particular problem statement over and over again, varying it just a little each time until you feel satisfied with the way you sound. Practicing frequently, but for only a few minutes at a time, works best. Five minutes is the *maximum* useful period for this kind of rehearsal.

If you practice in this way on a daily basis, it should only take a few weeks until you feel comfortable enough to say this kind of thing to a partner.

Please note: I am not in any way suggesting that you rehearse or memorize specific lines to be trotted out at some future date. You are instead rehearsing a general skill, and you will ultimately find that under the appropriate sexual circumstances, you will say whatever you wish to communicate, easily, comfortably, and spontaneously.

Now Do Yourself Some Favors

1. Do not read any further or do any other exercise until you have thoroughly done everything that I have asked you to do in this chapter.
2. Read to yourself, aloud and with feeling, your final list(s) of specific conditions, every day, until your problem is ancient history.
3. *Never* expect to be interested in sex or responsive during lovemaking unless most of your personal conditions are adequately met. As will be discussed later, provided you have the key sexual attitude (session 1), this does not in any way mean you can't usually make love when your conditions are not adequate.
4. Do whatever you can to have your conditions actually met as often as humanly possible. Don't just think about it, act upon it.

Chapter 8

Types of Sexual Drive Problems

Difficulties relating to, or deriving from, one's sexual drive divide logically into:

a. Problems of sexual *drive strength* and
b. Problems due to the object or activity toward which one's libido is directed (problems of *drive direction*).

Problems of Sexual Drive Strength

An excessively strong sexual drive may be a problem for the person possessed of it, and/or that individual's partner. This difficulty will be discussed in chapter 9.

A weak sexual drive or an apparently absent sexual interest may be a problem, once again, for the individual possessed of it, and/or for that person's partner. This difficulty may be "global" (affecting all areas of sexual expression) or "situational" (affecting only certain areas of sexual functioning). For example, some individuals have a strong desire for sexual activity with strangers, but none for the partner whom he or she loves. Both types of deficient sexual drive are discussed in chapter 11.

In many relationships, one sees two people, each with a perfectly normal sexual drive, where there is a major discrepancy in the strengths of their sexual drives. Depending on how this situation is handled, it may or may not cause difficulties. This problem of "mismatched libidos" is discussed in chapter 10.

Problems Due to the Direction of Sexual Drive

As will be discussed in chapter 18, non-monogamous desires are absolutely normal. This of course is not to suggest that individuals who do not experience such desires are in any way abnormal. If one experiences conflict about such desires, this constitutes a problem for the individual, and perhaps in consequence for any involved partner.

In normal heterosexuals, opposite-sex appropriate-aged partners are the individuals toward whom sexual drive is directed, while in normal homosexuals, it is aimed at appropriate-aged same-sex partners. With both normal heterosexuals and homosexuals, "normal" sexual activities are the goal. If one's sexual drive is consistently directed toward an inappropriate person (such as a child), or toward some socially unacceptable sexual behavior (such as public exhibition of the genitals), then a form of "deviant" sexual behavior is present. Such problems are beyond the scope of this work.

Chapter 9

Excessive Sexual Drive

As was mentioned in chapter 4, it is difficult to know just what constitutes an excessive sexual drive because of the extremely wide range of the normal libido. Certainly an habitual desire for sexual expression two or three times a day cannot be regarded as abnormal, although it may undoubtedly cause problems in a relationship. If an individual with a previously much lower habitual frequency of sexual interest develops a much greater libido, something must have happened, and this may very well indicate an abnormality for him or her. Perhaps the most practical yardstick of normality in persons with an habitually high libido is whether it causes life problems for them. For example, if so much time is devoted to sex that other areas of the individual's life suffer, then clearly a problem is present, and something may need to be done to relieve it.

The terms *satyriasis* and *nymphomania* are sometimes applied to excessive sexual drive in males and females respectively. It is important to realize that these labels refer only to behavior, which can result from many different influences. They do not describe specific entities! Popular literature has tended to glamourize excessive sexual drive, but in reality, more often than not, individuals possessed of an abnormally high libido are unhappy and often sexually unfulfilled.

Excessive (abnormal) sexual drive is mostly due to

1. Major psychiatric illness, especially hypomania, mania, and schizophrenia
2. Various disorders of the brain
3. Certain drugs
4. Personality problems

Compulsive Excessive Sexual Expression

In actual fact, the commonest cause of an abnormally high frequency of sexual expression is not a high sexual drive. Usually such behavior is an example of the nonsexual uses of sex, described in chapter 11. Many individuals are recurrently driven by complex psychological influences to a mounting inner (nonsexual) tension. If sexual activity is used in an attempt to relieve this, the person may ultimately become dependent on, or "addicted" to, repetitive sexual activity to release this tension. Since the real problem is not being addressed, the relief is only transitory, and the tension rapidly redevelops, motivating further sexual activity. This is not a sexual problem and certainly does not indicate the presence of an excessive sexual drive.

Management

None of the problems described in this chapter, sexual or otherwise, really lend themselves to truly effective self-management.

The treatment of true excessive sexual drive is essentially that of whatever actually causes the behavior, and usually requires professional assistance. There are available for reduction of an excessively high libido many commonly effective drugs of various types. However, such drugs are not always necessary, and always need to be complemented by other measures.

Chapter 10

The Problem of Mismatched Libidos

It is extremely common for the partners in a relationship to have different sexual appetites, either in the long term or from time to time. Just how this situation is handled often determines the quality of the couple's sexual interaction and frequently profoundly influences their overall relationship. We are here of course talking about a completely normal situation—the interaction of two people, each of whom has a perfectly normal but different interest in sex. Different sexual appetites based on an abnormally high or abnormally low libido are a separate issue, and here the basic management stratagem is, of course, to try to remedy the abnormality.

Effects of Normal but Mismatched Libidos

Handled appropriately, this situation causes no problems for either partner and, if anything, brings a couple closer. Mishandling due to a failure to understand the issues can have potentially serious adverse consequences. The guiding principle for avoiding problems is for both partners to have, or to develop, the *key sexual attitude* described in chapter 6 and now elaborated on.

The Key Sexual Attitude

When you really care about someone, you can always make love with them, unless your personal circumstances are unfavorable in the extreme. To elaborate, lovemaking means literally that—interacting physically and emotionally with someone you care for. Getting sexually aroused, having intercourse, and achieving orgasm are options and possible consequences during lovemaking, but are in no way essential. If you are lying down with your partner, fully clothed, holding each other, stroking nonsexual parts of the body, feeling close, and perhaps saying how you feel about each other, then by any reasonable standards you are making love, i.e., expressing love through a combination of intimate physical and emotional behaviors. Unless you are handicapped by sexual mythology, in this situation you will not feel that you or your partner must get aroused, must get into manipulation of overtly sexual parts of the body, must have intercourse, and must have orgasms.

Possession of this "key sexual attitude" is the secret to life-long sexual happiness and fulfillment in a relationship. If at this moment you don't genuinely have it and live it, you will be richly rewarded by working at developing it. See chapter 6 and appendix 1.

With this attitude, you can almost always make love together, unless one of you is really ill or feels absolutely dreadful. When you do make love with this attitude, there is no possible question of failure: lovemaking can only be successful.

Handling Sexual Situations in Relationships

First, at a given moment in time, both partners may simultaneously feel in the mood for sexual contact. There is no problem here, but it is very important to realize that this situation is uncommon other than in the very early stages of a relationship. If you really think about it, the likelihood of two people both simultaneously feeling an active need for sexual expression at precisely the same moment is slim.

The second situation is the usual one in most relationships, i.e., one partner feels like sexual expression and the other doesn't, although he or she doesn't feel any actual aversion to sexual contact. Under these circumstances, there is absolutely no reason at all why lovemaking should not proceed—the fact that one partner is not actively in the mood for sex is totally irrelevant if you both have the key sexual attitude. With caring physical caressing and an effective communication of feelings and needs, there is a very good chance that the originally disinterested partner will become actively interested, not that this is essential for making love. Obviously and importantly, for the "disinterested" partner, giving lovemaking a go under these circumstances is in no way a commitment to "go the whole way" and finish up having intercourse and orgasms. If at any stage this partner personally feels like going no further, then he or she will not do so, and will communicate this choice comfortably and without feeling bad about it. Under these circumstances, it is both caring and responsible for this partner to offer to relieve his or her mate's sexual tensions by some form of nonintercourse stimulation.

The third possible situation will occur from time to time in even the best relationships. Here, one partner is in the mood for lovemaking and the other actually feels actively opposed to personal involvement in sexual contact. This might, for example, be because he or she is very tired, feeling unwell, "uptight," or in some way indisposed. Any personal involvement in sexual activity for this partner at this time would be both stupid and actively unpleasant, and would run the risk of adversely affecting his or her future sexual responsiveness and pleasure. An unqualified "no" to one's partner's advances under these circumstances, however, is not the best way to handle this situation. Minimally, one's opposite number will feel somewhat rejected and that you don't need or appreciate their affection for you! Even worse consequences are hurt-sulking, noncommunication, or an argument. While we all have an absolute inviolable right to say no to an invitation to sexual contact, and should *never* say yes when we feel actively anti-sex (as opposed to neutral toward it), there are much better responses to a cared-for partner. More often than not under these "anti" circumstances one could, if one was prepared to make the effort and really cared about one's partner, offer to give him or her a brief massage, and manually or in some other way, such as with a vibrator, manipulate him or her to orgasm. To do so does not involve you in having to be fondled, get aroused, or perform in any way. You really have to be feeling pretty beat not to be physically able to manipulate your partner to orgasm. Of course, if you don't know or have never learned how to do this, it might be advisable to master this crucially important lovemaking skill under slightly better circumstances, such as when you don't feel "anti." Relieving your partner's sexual tensions under these circumstances is a particularly loving action, which brings you both closer and avoids all the various possible undesirable results of a simple no. Inevitably, however, you will sometimes feel so wretched that you just couldn't help your partner out even if your life depended on it. Lovingly communicating that difficulty, but without an apology, and framing it positively is the answer then. For example, you might say something like this: "Sweetheart, as much as I love you, today I feel so wretched I couldn't even offer to give you a hand-job. I'm sure I'll feel differently soon, and then it'll be good between us." In this model response, note the absence of an apology (since there is in reality nothing to apologize for) and that you are finishing up on a positive note.

While a sexually interested partner might be disappointed at this response, he or she couldn't really feel rejected or unloved. Masturbation to orgasm would then be a mature, sensible, natural way of relieving your sexual tension, should that feeling persist. Neither partner would of course feel any guilt whatsoever about this course of action.

When Mismatched Sexual Drives Persist

If the lower-libido partner habitually engages in sexual expression at a frequency greater than his or her natural or biological frequency, then he or she will probably *never* be aware of any spontaneous sexual interest, even though usually he or she will be responsive during lovemaking under adequate "conditions." This situation has been discussed in chapter 4.

When it becomes clear to a couple that their libidos are quite different, the crucial thing for them to do is to sit down and thoroughly discuss the issues, their respective feelings about the situation, and all the various possible options and handling strategies such as those described above in the various possible sexual situations. Attitudes and feelings about masturbation and extra-relationship sexual activity must be aired and clearly understood. Few individuals can cope satisfactorily with the actuality of their partner having sexual outlets with other people, and very often, if not usually, such outside involvements ultimately harm or destroy the primary relationship, even when they are conducted openly and by mutual agreement. Of course, there are occasional exceptions.

An essential skill needed to make any relationship really work is the ability and preparedness to make fair, mutually acceptable compromises. The sexual area is certainly no exception to this general rule.

A sensible thing to do when a couple have normal but mismatched libidos is to buy a vibrator (vibratory massager). With a little practice, most men and women can learn to reach orgasm quickly and pleasurably with this aid, and it can then be useful when one partner is aroused and wanting orgasm, and the other wishes to help out but is simply too tired or indisposed to offer a proficient "hand-job." The only *trap* to avoid is the too frequent use of the vibrator to produce orgasm. For women in particular, but even some men, if orgasm is too frequently produced by a vibrator, the ability to reach orgasm any other way may be lost, or it may become very difficult. Variety is the spice of lovemaking, so use your vibrator as an occasional variation, or when your partner is tired.

Mismatched Libidos: Abnormal States

If one partner has an abnormally high or deficient libido, then of course the thing to do is to tease out the causes of the problem and do something specific to overcome it, perhaps in difficult cases with professional help. While this is being achieved, some of the suggestions offered above may help.

Chapter 11

Deficient Sexual Desire: Do You Have This Problem?

As discussed in chapter 4, it is difficult to determine what is normal, which often makes deciding what is abnormal very complex indeed!

For the practical purpose of trying to help people, deficient sexual drive (DSD) is a problem needing attention only when it causes difficulties or unhappiness for the individual with it, or problems in his or her relationship with a partner, or both. Clearly normal but discrepant sexual desires are a separate issue, discussed in the previous chapter.

The Manifestations of Global DSD

The typical picture involves the following. There is an absence of a consciously experienced sexual need, a lack of interest in sexual matters, and an absence of thoughts or fantasies about sexual issues. In a sexual situation, genital stimulation will usually lead to no pleasure or sexual interest, although sometimes the purely physical sexual reflexes (lubrication, erection, orgasm, and ejaculation) may still function. These responses, if present, are not really satisfying. Pleasure, if any, is fleeting, perhaps occurring just around the time of orgasm and usually being limited to the genitals. Sexual activity tends to be avoided or engaged in for reasons other than desire, e.g., to avoid hurting a partner's feelings. There may be emotional discomfort, anxiety, and even panic in an intimate sexual situation with a partner, and aversive reactions to any form of touching.

The Manifestations of Situational DSD

Typically, the person feels desire and arousal in only certain situations, which for him or her are emotionally "safe." Sadly, it is usually toward the most appropriate partner that no desire or arousal is felt. For example, such an individual may have a strong desire for sexual activity with casual partners, but none at all for the partner whom he or she loves.

Some individuals in conflict about sexual expression with a loving, committed partner get around the problem in practice by fantasizing a different, safe sexual activity during lovemaking, for example, by pretending that their partner is a prostitute.

In the sexual situation with the "unsafe" partner, a person with situational DSD usually functions just like the individual with global DSD. In actual fact, the emotional discomfort and aversion may be even more severe.

Before making up your mind about whether you have one or other variety of DSD, let us consider other causes of sexual avoidance, which can be confused with DSD, but where there is no actual libido problem.

The Main Causes of Sexual Avoidance of One's Partner

1. Lack of interest in sex, with or without sexual aversion (chapter 14)
   - global DSD
   - situational DSD.
2. Fear of pregnancy or venereal disease.
3. Sexual phobias of various types (chapters 12, 18).
4. Fears of intimacy and commitment, or of success, or of experiencing pleasure (chapter 12).
5. Deliberate withholding, for example, to punish the partner.
6. Embarrassment and anxiety over a sexual dysfunction such as impotence.
7. Dislike for, or lack of interest in, the partner.
8. Dislike of the partner's habitual style of lovemaking.
9. Preoccupation with nonsexual concerns.
10. Physical pain induced by, or associated with, sexual contact.

Note that most of these separate problems can go on to induce a frank sexual drive difficulty with time.

Nonsexual Uses of Sex

Paradoxically, some people actually have DSD when they in fact frequently engage in sexual activity! Here, sex is being used for nonsexual purposes, such as:

to relieve a nonsexual tension;
to relieve boredom;
because they feel it is expected;
to dominate, hurt, or control a partner;
to relieve insomnia;
to get pregnant;
for material gain;
to prove one's masculinity or femininity;
to be reassured of one's attractiveness;
to obtain love and affection, or even simply attention.

It may at first glance seem strange that people would engage in sex for reasons that really have nothing to do with sexual interest! However, the facts are that for large numbers of people, much of the time their sexual participation has got nothing whatever to do with a strictly sexual need. If you think about your own sexual behavior, you should be able to see how this has applied to you, at least sometimes.

If you can identify with either of the patterns of *true DSD* (global or situational) described above, and it concerns you or causes problems in your relationship with your partner, then you should benefit by carefully following the program to which the rest of this book is devoted.

Chapter 12

What You Need To Know About the Causes of Deficient Sexual Desire

Most frequently, deficient sexual desire (DSD) is due not to one single cause, but to *a variety of factors acting together*, no one of these by itself being responsible for the problem.

Contributory causes can for convenience be divided into three groups:

1. chemical agents
2. physical diseases
3. psychological factors

Chemical Agents as Contributory Causes of DSD

Some chemicals used in industry and agriculture, some illicit drugs, and many drugs prescribed by doctors can contribute to the development and maintenance of DSD.

If a person with DSD is exposed to particular chemicals in his or her work or hobbies, he or she could check with a government or university department of occupational health to find out whether the agents concerned could possibly have any effect on sexual drive. If they could, appropriate measures to prevent exposure are indicated. In actual fact, however, very few industrial chemicals to which men and women are exposed are known to contribute to DSD.

Many prescribed drugs can induce or contribute to a decrease in sexual drive in some people. No drug always causes DSD in every person exposed to the doses used in medicine. In fact, with most drugs capable of inducing DSD, this side effect occurs in only a small percentage of those taking it. Why this occurs is usually not well understood, but sometimes it is due to the drug adding to the effect of another preexisting contributory factor, the combination leading to DSD. Some people simply appear to be more susceptible to this particular side effect. The drugs known to contribute to DSD, at least occasionally, are many and varied, and include some (but certainly not all) blood pressure lowering drugs, tranquilizers, and antidepressants. If you are taking any drug and have DSD, check with your doctor as to whether it has ever been found to contribute to DSD. If he doesn't know, he can look up its published side effects or contact the drug company who markets the drug, who would certainly know. You must clearly understand, however, that just because a drug you are taking can sometimes contribute to DSD, this does not in any way mean it is involved in your problem of DSD! The only way to be sure is to stop the drug (if that is medically advisable, which only your doctor can decide) or change to one that will give you the same benefit, but hopefully not contribute to DSD.

Illicit or "street" drugs can all decrease libido, at least in certain individuals. This is true even of those drugs that occasionally enhance sexual interest. See chapter 18.

Alcohol has important effects on sexual drive. In relatively small doses, it may appear to increase sexual drive or interest in some individuals. If this occurs, it is due to a release of some psychological inhibition, usually based on anxiety. The usual response to a small dose of alcohol is no discernible effect on sexual drive or interest, although some few individuals find that even small amounts can inhibit their sexual interest. As the dose of alcohol consumed progressively increases, so usually does one's sexual drive decrease. Chronic heavy abuse of alcohol commonly contributes to a sustained loss of sexual drive.

Because hormonal preparations are very widely used as oral contraceptives, a few words about their possible effects on libido are in order. There is no doubt in clinical practice that many women given certain oral contraceptive preparations experience a decrease in libido. Whether this effect operates at a physiological or a psychological level, or both, is often uncertain, since it is clearly an individual response. Some of these women find that their libido is restored when they change to a differently formulated oral contraceptive. For many women, of course, the oral contraceptive pill has no significant effect on their sexual drive. For other women, some of these preparations are associated with an increase in libido. Whether this is a physiological response, or a psychological reaction to the relief of fear of an unwanted pregnancy, or some combination of these factors is not clear. If a woman who has been taking an oral contraceptive preparation for some considerable time without ill effect subsequently experiences a change in libido, logic suggests that it is probably not involved in causation.

If there is any question that an oral contraceptive has led to a decrease in libido, it is worthwhile experimenting to see if a different preparation can be found which does not have this effect before considering alternative forms of contraception.

Physical Diseases as Contributory Causes of DSD

A large number of diverse physical disorders can contribute to DSD. This may be via a specific effect upon the body mechanisms regulating sexual drive, or it may represent an indirect response due to impaired general health or painful sex.

Diseases exerting a relatively specific effect usually do so by involvement of the endocrine (hormone) system, or the brain, or both. Some of these disorders are, or can become, quite serious if left untreated and may need medical attention.

A larger number of physical disorders indirectly adversely affect libido, most often by interfering with one's "conditions" for being sexually interested. Particularly relevant here are chronic, painful, and debilitating or disabling conditions. However, even if the contribution of these disorders to DSD can't be overcome directly, usually a great deal can be done to override their adverse effects on libido by meticulous attention to getting all of one's other conditions adequately met. Another mechanism by which physical disorders can indirectly contribute to DSD is by causing pain during, or in association with, sexual contact. This might be, for example, by inducing painful intercourse, painful orgasm, painful ejaculation, or by bringing on heart pain (angina).

Psychological Factors Contributing to DSD

Psychological issues may contribute to DSD by acting as predisposing factors, inducing or precipitating factors, or as maintaining factors. For convenience of description, I have chosen to lump these various issues together, and divide them simply (and sometimes arbitrarily) into personal and relationship contributions.

Personal Issues

A wide range of factors can be involved, often acting in combination. Only the most common and/or important will be considered. These will first be listed (although very arbitrarily, since there is much overlap), then discussed.

Checklist of Common Personal Psychological Issues

- Psychological stress
- Psychiatric illness, especially a depressive illness
- Unrealistic expectations
- Poor self-image
- Sexual boredom
- Repeated ungratifying sexual experiences
- Performance anxiety
- Excessive concern with pleasing the partner
- Actively trying to be sexually interested and aroused
- Anxiety and guilt about sex and pleasure
- Fear of venereal disease
- Fear of unwanted pregnancy
- Fear of having a heart attack, or some other medical problem
- Specific traumatic events
- Irrational perceived dangers
- Nonspecific dysphoria (negative mood)
- Irrational anger
- The "automatic turnoff mechanism"
- Distrust
- Fear of intimacy and commitment
- Sexual phobias
- Sexual dysfunctions
- Infertility

Psychological Stress

One's libido is often exquisitely sensitive to stress of different kinds. Usually, under stress there is a reduction in perceived sexual drive, and it may even seem to disappear completely. In some individuals, however, stress, apparently paradoxically, leads to an increase in the frequency of sexual expression. In such cases, sex is really being used either for relief of nonsexual tensions or as a way of achieving the needed comfort and security of extra closeness with a loved one.

Surprising though it may seem, some people who are chronically stressed and emotionally drained as a consequence don't appreciate what is going on, perhaps because it has become a way of life. They apparently fail to appreciate that the cumulative effect of many individual, relatively trivial events or chronic long hours of work can be enormous.

Psychiatric Illness

A variety of psychiatric illnesses can lead to a decrease in sexual drive, just as do many nonspecific physical illnesses. By far the most common and important, however, is what is called a depressive illness. This is a somewhat complex matter, as you do not actually have to feel particularly depressed to have this ailment! The recognition of this very common psychological disorder is discussed in chapter 16. Libido is often restored to normal simply by treating this illness.

Unrealistic Expectations

Many people believe that they should be able to be sexually interested and experience spontaneous libido despite unfavorable personal circumstances. As previously discussed, the facts are that we all have our own individual and often idiosyncratic conditions which must be met at least reasonably well before there is much chance of us being interested in sex or sexually responsive.

These unrealistic expectations often lead to adverse consequences and the creation of vicious circles, perpetuating DSD. For example, once an individual begins to worry about his or her "decreased" libido, because it is erroneously perceived as abnormal, this worry in itself often tends further to suppress sexual drive strength. Alternatively, some persons may, despite a decreased libido due to adverse circumstances, nonetheless attempt to continue sexual expression for essentially nonsexual reasons—for example, to "do the right thing" by the partner, to prove they can still do "it," to relieve nonsexual tension, or to get attention or affection. The usual result here is dissatisfaction with performance, lack of pleasure, and then increasing anxiety about the lack of sexual interest or pleasure, compounding the problem.

Poor Self-image

If you don't like yourself much or have little confidence in yourself as a person, this can interfere with your sexual interest in a variety of ways. You will probably not see yourself as attractive to your partner, erotically competent, or even as very lovable. When you do encounter any difficulty with sex, this will tend to aggravate your self-esteem problem, so that vicious circles are easily set up.

Your poor self-image may mainly relate to your physical appearance—you may feel you are unattractive because of excessive weight, wrinkles, surgical scars, and the like. Concerns like these can profoundly affect your interest in and comfort during sexual relating.

Sexual Boredom

A very important, simple, and often ignored factor underpinning some cases of DSD is sexual boredom. No matter how much a couple are in love and how physically attracted to each other they may be, when their lovemaking has been repeated several thousand times, often in the same bed, at roughly the same time, using commonly a rather stereotyped or at best limited range of erotic manipulations, some fall in sexual appetite is inevitable. It is rather akin to eating exactly the same meal, every day, at the same time, in the same environment—no matter how much the particular food is intrinsically desired, there will be a decrease in interest in it. Attention to these simple factors can often reawaken declining sexual interest. Unhappily, it is not at all uncommon for partners to react to what is really simple sexual boredom, as though there was something major wrong with the marriage or the partner or themselves. This misperception may sometimes have serious consequences, such as marital breakdown and depression. It is one of the common causes of the "affair," which usually ultimately worsens the marital situation and sexual desire for the spouse.

Repeated Ungratifying Sexual Experiences
This is a common cause of progressively declining libido, particularly when individuals are committed to sexually insensitive partners, both male and female. One often sees this also in women who remain unable to achieve orgasm despite an initial ability to be interested and responsive. It is as though the individual unconsciously suppresses awareness of sexual desire as a way of avoiding repeated disappointment and frustration.

Performance Anxiety
It is not at all uncommon to see sexual desire inhibited when anxiety about sexual performance emerges. Rather than face possible self-perceived "failure," the individual consciously or unconsciously suppresses awareness of sexual drive.

Excessive Concern With Pleasing the Partner
Some individuals, most commonly performance-orientated men, are so preoccupied during lovemaking with pleasing and satisfying their partner, tasks for which they erroneously believe they are totally responsible, that they ignore and/or become unaware of their own responses and arousal. If their partner colludes with this and adopts an habitually passive role during lovemaking, the sexual drive of the offending person may suffer progressively.

Active Trying
Some individuals with DSD who are concerned about the problem commit the error of actively trying to force themselves to become sexually interested and aroused. This is one of the worst things they could do, because such forcing usually ultimately leads to the problem becoming worse!

Anxiety and Guilt About Sex and Pleasure
There are many men and women whose upbringing has taught them to feel anxious and/or guilty about sexual expression and/or about experiencing pleasure for themselves. If their subsequent life experiences have not enabled them to overcome this faulty learning, the result as an adult can be DSD. Even in this era of so-called sexual liberation, many unfortunate people in the community, of all ages, labor under severe burdens of anxiety and guilt about normal sexual expression.

Fear of Venereal (Sexually Transmitted) Disease
A legitimate concern about picking up VD may effectively inhibit libido in circumstances where such an infection is a real possibility. Some people, however, have an irrational fear of contracting VD. This irrational fear, sometimes called venereophobia, can contribute to DSD.

Fear of Unwanted Pregnancy
In certain individuals, a perfectly understandable fear of an unwanted pregnancy exists because of the absence for various reasons of effective contraception. This can contribute to DSD. Some people even irrationally fear an unwanted pregnancy despite the proper use of effective contraception!

Fear of Heart Attack or Other Medical Problems
Many people have disease of the coronary (heart) arteries, and have chest pain on exertion (angina), or have had a heart attack. Some of these people irrationally fear that sexual activity will cause a heart attack, and this fear can contribute to a genuine decrease in libido (as well as simple sexual avoidance!). It is very rare indeed for this type of heart disease legitimately to contraindicate mutually satisfying lovemaking, intercourse, and orgasm. If this possibility is something that concerns you, talk over the issues with a specialist cardiologist, who should be able to give you very specific advice and reassurance!

Sometimes DSD is based on fears of other possible adverse medical consequences of sexual activity, such as damaging an unborn baby, precipitating a stroke, or a seizure, or breathlessness, and so on. Almost always these fears are exaggerated or unrealistic, and informed medical advice can go a long way to reduce them.

Specific Traumatic Events
Specific traumatic events can sometimes induce DSD. One sometimes sees this, for example, after an anonymous rape, even when the partner is very supportive and considerate and doesn't press his sexual intentions. The woman usually consciously wants to enjoy sex again with her partner, but the trauma has effectively blocked her ability to experience sexual desire. This situation is also sometimes seen as a persistent problem in the wake of the discovery that one's partner has been having an affair. It is also common after incestuous contact, or other anxiety- and guilt-provoking sexual experiences, even from early childhood.

Irrational Perceived Dangers
It is normal for sexual desire to be inhibited in the face of real danger, but in many individuals it is inhibited because of irrational and false perceived dangers. Sexual situations that are in reality perfectly safe, may nonetheless be seen as dangerous on the basis of past experiences. The actual relevant past events are many and varied, and may have led to an irrational fear of physical injury, abuse, exploitation, rejection, losing control, and so on.

Nonspecific Dysphoria
Any unpleasant or negative mood state such as anxiety, anger, guilt, shame, or disgust, even when it results from causes totally unrelated to sex, can interfere with sexual drive or interest. This operates in much the same way as a physical illness that nonspecifically interferes with sexual

drive by making one's conditions for being sexually interested and responsive unfavorable.

Irrational Anger

Consciously experienced anger is incompatible with simultaneous sexual desire in most people. In some individuals with DSD, anger is irrationally triggered by some aspect of the partner, the relationship, or the sexual situation, which activates negative associations from the past, not necessarily consciously appreciated. For example, a woman who had a very controlling, dominating father may become irrationally angry when sex with her husband is a possibility, because at some level sex is seen as an expression of his dominance and her submission. At a conscious level, such a woman may appear to be angry over some trivial, superficial perceived deficiency in her partner. The repetitive and irrational nature of her anger, whenever sex is a possibility, is a pointer to what may really be going on.

The Automatic Turnoff Mechanism

Many people with DSD *automatically* and without deliberation get themselves into a negative emotional state whenever a sexual opportunity arises. They have negative thoughts, memories, or mental images that cause them to feel angry, fearful, or distracted, thus effectively suppressing the emergence of sexual desire. Some focus automatically on an unattractive feature of themselves or their partner, or a memory of a past wrongdoing or deficiency may be employed.

The mechanism usually operates unconsciously (i.e., not deliberately), automatically, and involuntarily. The individual usually fails to appreciate what he or she is actually doing, instead often tending to see himself or herself as poorly done by. The hard facts are, of course, that if we try, we can usually control and select just what aspect of a person or situation we become involved with, this naturally heavily influencing the quality of the experience for us. A normal person, of course, does exactly the opposite to the individual with an automatic turnoff. He or she does not allow negative thoughts or distractions to intrude on a sexual situation. Such a person focuses on the partner's positive features and ignores the negative, behavior which maximizes sexual pleasure.

This commonly observed turnoff mechanism is merely a final common pathway through which diverse psychological influences operate. It is extremely important to practice, however, because it is very susceptible to a direct attack in treatment.

Distrust

If one's partner is not trusted, for realistic reasons or because of past unhappy experiences with others, it may be difficult to let go of emotional over-control and abandon oneself to sexual pleasure. To do so generates frightening feelings of vulnerability, blocking off sexual desire.

Fear of Intimacy and Commitment

There are many individuals who for various reasons are consciously or unconsciously fearful of a close and intimate involvement and commitment. *The closer to the partner he or she becomes emotionally, the greater the anxiety.* This in turn inhibits sexual desire, thus effectively reducing closeness (and sometimes eventually destroying the relationship). This situation tends to recur, and one sees in successive involvements a normal sexual interest in the early nonintimate stages of the relationship, decreasing as greater closeness and the possibility or commitment are achieved. There are, of course, other possible causes of this pattern of behavior.

Sexual Phobias

A phobia is a persistent and irrational fear of a specific object, activity, or situation, inducing a compelling desire to avoid whatever is feared. The affected person recognizes that the fear is excessive or unreasonable.

An element of irrational anxiety about sexual expression, associated with a degree of some form of sexual avoidance, is present in many sexual disorders, although it is often secondary to them and of much lesser importance. Sometimes, however, phobic anxiety about some aspect of normal sexual behavior is a dominant feature of a sexual problem. The afflicted individual may, because of anxiety, avoid all forms of sexual expression, including the experiencing of sexual desire, thoughts or fantasies, masturbation, and any form of interpersonal contact.

More often, the anxiety and associated avoidance behavior is confined to specific areas of sexual expression. For example, there may be anxiety limited to having sexual thoughts and feelings, or restricted to looking at or touching the genitals, or to sexual odors or secretions, or to various lovemaking options such as kissing, oral-genital contact, intercourse, or to having an orgasm. A morbid dread of one's sexual performance being inadequate, or of pregnancy, are also seen.

Some severe sexual phobias lead to sexual avoidance, which may be mistaken for lack of sexual interest. Others may cause a secondary decrease in or lack of interest in sex. Some individuals have a specific fear of actually experiencing sexual drive or interest.

Certain other aspects of the common and important problem of sexual phobias will be discussed in chapter 18.

Sexual Dysfunctions

When for some reason an individual has, or develops, some disorder of effective sexual functioning (most commonly impotence, premature or retarded ejaculation in the male, and orgasm disorders and painful or difficult intercourse in the female), there may be a secondary decrease in sexual drive or interest. This may be for various reasons such as performance anxiety, feelings of inadequacy, repeated ungratifying sexual experiences, and so on. When this occurs, the primary sexual difficulty is usually made worse, establishing a vicious cycle of progressively deteriorating sexual interest and function. Of course, these other sexual problems may be a consequence, rather than a cause, of DSD.

Sometimes DSD in one partner appears to be largely a psychological reaction to a sexual dysfunction in his or her mate. One often sees this, for example, in a woman whose partner develops chronic erectile impotence. It is as if the women "switches off" awareness of her sexual nature when her husband keeps avoiding sex because of his humiliation over his impotency, or when lovemaking is repeatedly unsatisfying because of it.

Infertility
For an individual who very much desires a child, his or her emotional reaction to infertility (personal or partner's) may inhibit sexual drive.

Relationship Issues

Once again, a wide range of factors can be involved, usually acting together with other adverse influences to produce or maintain the end result—DSD. The most common issues will first be listed, then discussed.

Checklist of Common Relationship Issues

- Lack of knowledge about proper erotic technique
- Partner adherence to behavior controlled by sexual myths
- Mismatched libidos
- Lack of loving feelings toward one's partner
- Marital conflict
- Unrealistic and therefore unmet expectations
- Failure to communicate sexual and emotional needs
- Perceived nonsexual use of sex
- Inappropriate transference of childish expectations onto the partner
- Inappropriate partner responses to sexual problems

Lack of Knowledge About Proper Erotic Technique
If one's partner is unsophisticated about lovemaking and despite gentle (or not so gentle!) hints can't or won't make the effort to improve things, this may impair one's libido. This situation is, of course, one cause of repeated ungratifying sexual experiences, discussed above.

A more subtle variation on this theme is when the partner's erotic technique is passable until the changes of ageing necessitate a little more. When this is not forthcoming, often because the partner simply doesn't know what is necessary, lovemaking may go into a decline, and DSD can be the result. For example, many women never fondle their partner's penis during lovemaking. This may be okay when a man is young, but in his 50s (or sooner) he usually needs direct penile stimulation to erect adequately. If this is not forthcoming because of a lack of knowledge, commonly in both partners, erectile "problems" set in, often being followed by DSD.

Adherence to Behavior Controlled by Sexual Myths
Often lovemaking is less than satisfactory because the erotic behavior of one (or both) partners is controlled by destructive myths. For example, one of the commonest is the misconception, shared by many men and women, that "sex is all up to the man." If one's partner adheres to this myth, sex for the man can eventually become ungratifying, and DSD can be the result.

Mismatched libidos
This common situation has been discussed in detail in chapter 10. For our present purposes, not two things:

1. Habitual sexual expression at a rate greater than one's natural rhythm may result in a total absence of any consciously perceived interest in sex, even though lovemaking may be enjoyable and fulfilling.
2. If the mismatch is *mishandled,* then there may be a progressive loss of sexual interest, in either partner, but most commonly in the person with the lower libido.

Lack of Loving Feelings Toward One's Partner
For many people, loving, tender feelings toward one's partner are a necessary prerequisite for the experiencing of sexual desire toward them. If for one reason or other you do not love your partner at all, or enough, or just for the moment, sexual interest may be inhibited. This, of course, certainly does not apply to everyone—some people, more often men, lust after their partner even when they actually dislike them!

Marital Conflict
All relationships have problems from time to time, and when this occurs, conflict may arise between partners. Very often under these circumstances there is an early decrease in or loss of sexual interest, primarily because essential conditions are not being met. Of course, in some relationships, deliberate deprivation of sex is used as a way to hurt the partner, and this must not be confused with loss of sexual interest.

Unrealistic and Therefore Unmet Expectations
Even though we are usually not consciously aware of it, we bring to marriage a series of expectations about what men and women do and do not do, what sex should be like, and so on. Many of these expectations are both idealistic and unrealistic. In the sexual arena we tend to expect perfect sex and that our partner will naturally be the perfect lover, all this without much practice, or often even very basic sexual knowledge. The trouble is that when these usually unspoken expectations are unfulfilled, we become unhappy, disenchanted, or angry. These reactions can potently disturb our ability to be aware of our sexual drive, or can channel that interest away from our spouse to other potential or actual partners who, at least in the short term, are perceived as more adequately able to meet our expectations.

Unmet, undiscussed, and unrealistic expectations are one of the commonest sources of relationship difficulties, the ultimate problem, of course, boiling down to a failure of effective communication!

Failure To Communicate Sexual and Emotional Needs
Part of the pervasive mythology about lovemaking is that if your partner really loves you, he or she will automatically know what you want and don't want. It sounds absurd when it is written down like this, but I assure you that many couples act as if they truly believed this. The hard facts are that our sexual needs change from time to time, even from moment to moment, and even the most caring and concerned partner can't read our mind! In the sexual situation, each partner must clearly communicate his or her needs and wishes. Most don't, and then wonder why sex is less than totally rewarding! Unsatisfactory sex tends to decrease libido. Whatever way you look at it, effective communication is a key issue!

Perceived Nonsexual Uses of Sex
As discussed in chapter 11, sexual behavior is often engaged in for reasons that have nothing to do with satisfying a sexual need!

When the individual on the receiving end of repeated sexual activity that is not motivated by love and sexual desire wakes up to what is happening, there is commonly an understandable decrease in enthusiasm for sexual contact, at least with that partner.

Inappropriate Transference of Childish Expectations
Some people never really grow up, and when they marry, simply transfer to their partner the role their parents fulfilled for them. While this may actually suit some spouses who relish the maternal or paternal role, most of us want and expect to relate in marriage to an adult. We do not expect habitually to have to do for our spouse what a parent usually does for a loved child. When we don't behave like a good parent, a child-like spouse becomes angry and resentful, and this emotional reaction can kill off libido. The partner who declines to behave like a parent may also lose interest in sexual relating, at least with the child-spouse.

Inappropriate Partner Responses to Sexual Problems
In the field of sex therapy, there is a rule of thumb to which one does not often see exceptions. It goes like this: With any sexual problem in either sex, the partner's response to it usually makes it worse, even in loving and caring relationships.

The reason is simple enough: few spouses are saintly enough to avoid feeling at least occasional disappointment or displeasure when their partner fails to "deliver the goods" sexually. Unfortunately, these inevitable negative responses aggravate the original sexual difficulty.

Of course, less caring partners may be much more consistently and overtly negative, and such responses rapidly and profoundly aggravate sexual difficulties, especially the spouse's ability to experience sexual interest.

In my clinical experience, this problem of inappropriate partner responses is *so common, so important, and so destructive* that it will be elaborated on in some detail, using two typical examples.

Scenario 1: A man with a healthy sexual appetite and a basically sound relationship with a wife with a reasonably matched libido goes through an extended period of considerable stress in his occupation. Believing that sharing his worries with his wife will only cause her to worry unnecessarily and also suffer, he does not unburden himself to her, or only does so infrequently and to a limited degree. As a normal consequence of the stress, his sexual appetite decreases; he doesn't understand why, but is initially perhaps too preoccupied to think much about it. His spouse perceives an unhappy, preoccupied, rather withdrawn partner who is no longer very interested in her sexually. She then personalizes much of the situation, interpreting his overall behavior (the real origins of which she does not understand) as being due to dissatisfaction with her, lack of love for her, rejection of her, and so on. She then reacts self-protectively by emotional withdrawal, compounding the problem, because more than ever he really needs her support. She may initially try to get him interested in lovemaking, using all sorts of ploys, but quits after a time because at best she gets a detached mechanical response, at worst sexual refusal. Eventually she avoids self-protectively any effort at sexual involvement, because the consequences are too upsetting and damaging to her self-esteem. She then begins to suppress her libido, because awareness of it merely generates problems for her.

Meanwhile, the man perceives his wife as increasingly distant and sexually disinterested. When the couple have had no sexual contact for some time, each is too anxious and embarrassed to try initiating it, fearing rejection or an angry outburst. Over this time the relationship has often been steadily deteriorating. Each partner is becoming more and more displeased with his or her opposite number, reacting to undesired behaviors in ways that reinforce (increase) them so that a satisfactory climate for lovemaking or the generation of sexual feelings does not arise. The situation may be further compounded by affairs, alcohol abuse, depression, and so on. If either partner has an affair, whatever the outcome sexually, the relationship will usually be worse off. If the sexual side of the outside relationship is good, the marital situation becomes even less tolerable and the partner tends to be blamed. If it is unsuccessful, e.g., if the man cannot perform or gets little other than tension release, or if the woman is unresponsive or anorgasmic, their respective self-esteems are further damaged, and the chances of resurrecting the sexual side of the marriage decrease even further. Even though at some stage in the longitudinal history of this scenario the original causes of the man's loss of libido disappeared, the system now established acts against any chance of recovery. The couple may divorce, work out some tolerable asexual compromise, living out their lives much less satisfyingly than otherwise might be possible, or they may seek help.

The exact details of the scenario are almost infinitely variable, but the dynamics are the same—initial loss of libido as a predictable normal response to stress, illness, or medication; failure by the couple to communicate adequately about the situation and to understand it; and progressive responses to the overall situation, making it steadily worse. The couple's system maintains the DSD, even when the initial precipitating factors have disappeared.

Scenario 2: A very common female variation on this theme occurs after childbirth. The woman is tired, getting inadequate and frequently interrupted sleep, is often worried about her handling of the new child, unsure about the significance of its crying, and so on. She may also at some level resent what the child has done to her previously ordered and satisfying life, and then feel guilty about her reaction. She may also be a little depressed, and the hormonal changes associated with lactation may contribute to the other factors causing her absent libido. Her husband may be initially supportive, help with the housework and child care, and not push his sexual attentions. After a while, however, he begins to react adversely to the changes in his life and in his wife and spends more time "doing his own thing" outside the house, perhaps losing himself in the furtherance of his career, or drowning his dissatisfactions in alcohol. When he attempts lovemaking, he may be flatly rejected, leading to anger or feelings of no longer being loved. He may then come to resent the child, seeing it as a competitor for his wife's attentions. She may, against her basic wishes and sometimes with considerable resentment, copulate with him out of a sense of duty or to stop his incessant hounding of her for sexual contact. Her sexual participation under these circumstances is an aversive event, which can further suppress her libido or act against its spontaneous recovery. Additionally, when she does have intercourse, for the wrong reasons, it may hurt because her genitals have yet to recover fully, and because lubrication is inadequate since she is not aroused. She may worry at her own lack of responsiveness and feel resentful at his pleasure and orgasm, contasted with her own misery. He reacts sooner or later to her poorly disguised disinterest during copulation as indicating that he is no longer loved, or that she no longer finds him sexually attractive. Self-defensively he may then withdraw emotionally, or obsessively pressure her for sex and sexual variety.

Whatever the couple does seems to wind up making things worse, because each responds to displeasing behavior in the mate in ways that ultimately reinforce (increase) it. After a time the problem becomes entrenched and self-perpetuating, even though the original causative factors have ceased to operate. Once again the basic fault was failure of adequate communication early on, compounded by responses that progressively aggravated the resulting difficulties. The results are often tragic in the extreme, the more so because they are unnecessary.

A Trap About Relationship Issues and Sexual Problems

While it is obvious and indisputable that relationship difficulties can cause or aggravate sexual problems, sometimes a couple collude to mislabel basic relationship deficiencies as sexual problems. They say, in essence, "our relationship generally is great, our only problems are in the sexual area," when this is in fact far from the truth. Of course, sometimes this evaluation *is* absolutely true.

If your sexual problems don't seem to be responding to your joint best efforts to follow the program in this book, it could be that sex isn't the real issue! When other, more basic relationship problems get mislabelled as sexual ones, it is very difficult indeed to improve both the sexual interaction and the real underlying issues.

Chapter 13

Male and Female Reactions to Deficient Sexual Desire

A man's response to his own lack of sexual interest is very variable. It is influenced by whether or not he had previously been much more interested, his previous satisfaction during lovemaking, his age, his general health, the true quality of his relationship with his partner, the partner's attitude to the problem, and many other variables.

In general, men tend to be less concerned about this problem than they are about erectile difficulties. They may be more puzzled as to why than actually worried, especially if their partner isn't fussed about the situation. Of course, some men react extremely adversely to any change in this overvalued body function because their concept of themselves as a man is very much tied to their sexuality! They may react to DSD with anger, depression, anxiety, guilt, shame, etc. Drugs may be resorted to in an effort to flog their libido along. Obviously, all these responses tend to make their problem of DSD *much worse,* regardless of what caused it in the first place. Other men passively accept the situation, erroneously believing that this is a normal and inevitable consequence of ageing. This is particularly likely when their partner subscribes to the same myth.

Some men seem to think their DSD must indicate that they no longer love their partner or find her attractive. They are likely to put the matter to the test with another partner, usually ultimately making the sexual situation within the relationship worse, whatever the sexual outcome outside the relationship.

Certain men have found it convenient to blame others for previous personal difficulties, and when afflicted with DSD, this blaming tendency is carried over into the sexual area. They accuse their partner of not being interested in sex, or of being sexually inadequate or unattractive or whatever, as a way of trying to preserve their own self-esteem! Naturally, spouses object to this, and the sexual difficulty worsens, as may the relationship generally.

As a broad generalization then, almost any reaction a man can have to his DSD will aggravate the problem.

Men's reactions to DSD in their partner likewise run the gamut from indifference to concerned help, to anxiety, to feeling rejected and unloved, to blaming, and so on. Some men strongly personalize the situation, and feel they must be unattractive to their partner. This reaction can lead to endlessly repeated, almost obsessive attempts to interest the partner (usually alienating her), or to a faddish preoccupation with health and appearance, or to outside sexual relationships designed to prove they really are sexually attractive. Some drown their misery in alcohol, others simply give up, colluding with their partner to avoid sexual contact.

Understandably, if your partner has situational DSD (chapter 11) and only lacks interest in you, this can be a particularly bitter pill to swallow if you know about it!

As another broad generalization, almost any response a man can make to his partner's DSD, even if it is usually supportive and caring, tends to aggravate his partner's DSD. Even supportive, loving responses can worsen the problem, by making a woman feel guilty that she is letting down such a caring, wonderful partner. It is almost a no-win situation for both partners!

Women's reactions to their own DSD are phenomenologically similar to men's, although "not caring" is apparently much more common. Extreme reactions are also much less frequently seen. As with her male counterpart, however, almost any reaction a woman can have to her own DSD will tend to make it worse.

Women's reactions to their partners' DSD tend to be much stronger than to their own, perhaps because of a tendency to personalize the situation, for example, to react as if the partner's DSD indicates that he does not love her, does not find her attractive, etc. Even paranoid responses may occur: the woman believing in, and/or accusing her husband of, sexual involvement outside the relationship. The same spectrum of responses is seen as described above for men. As before, the woman's response to her partner's difficulty usually makes it worse, even in caring and loving relationships!

Is There Any Way of Avoiding This No-Win Situation?

If a couple are both wedded to the key sexual attitude (chapter 10) and practice what they believe, handling the various possible sexual contingencies between them as described in chapter 10, then neither partner's reactions to a problem of DSD should make it worse. This observation hopefully underscores yet again the *crucial* importance of developing the key sexual attitude.

Another Important Generalization About DSD

By far the most crucial factor influencing the outcome of the treatment of DSD is the true quality of a person's relationship with his or her partner. It is sometimes amazing how even very severe and difficult problems can be overcome in the context of an extremely good relationship.

If you don't have a partner, please do not in any way interpret this last statement as meaning that without one you cannot overcome your problem, as this is certainly not true! It is a fact, however, that if you do have a partner, and he or she is other than loving, caring, and truly cooperative, your task will be much more difficult.

It should by now be crystal clear that when a person with DSD has a partner, it is not just his or her problem, but their problem. A logical consequence of this insight is that when a person with DSD has a partner, that partner simply must be actively involved in any treatment program. Without your partner's *willing* participation and cooperation, there are limitations on what any therapist or treatment can achieve. If your partner is actively uncooperative, you have little chance of being interested in sex with him or her until and unless his or her attitudes and behavior can be modified.

Chapter 14

Sexual Aversion

What Are We Talking About?

Sexual aversion is a difficulty that goes beyond just a decrease in, or absence of, sexual interest, although this is part of the problem. It is a persistent avoidance of sexual contact and any physical touching that could possibly lead on to sex, associated with an *automatic negative emotional response* (most commonly anxiety or anger) to sex, or the possibility of sex.

Who Gets This Problem?

It is more frequently seen in women than in men, and is in essence a fairly common complication of DSD.

What Are the Manifestations of Sexual Aversion?

1. A decrease in, or absence of, sexual desire.
2. A decrease in, or absence of, nonsexual affectionate touching with the partner.
3. Physical contact that could possibly lead to sex (or even all physical contact) leads to tension, anxiety, irritation, or anger.

4. Avoidance of all situations that could possibly lead to sexual contact. Common ploys are: becoming exceedingly busy, going to bed early or very late, having relatives or friends constantly around, provoking an argument around bedtime, and so on.

5. Progressively less frequent actual sexual contact. Sex may be engaged in episodically (but progressively less frequently) to relieve one's biological sexual urge (until even that is suppressed), or more usually to relieve *an escalating sense of guilt.* Surprisingly, sometimes when the aversive person gets into a sexual situation with the partner (for all the wrong reasons!), he or she may actually be responsive and even achieve orgasm. As the problem progressively worsens, all sexual contact with the partner may cease.

6. Both partners often feel unloved and rejected, and frequently open conflict and arguments develop around these issues. Marital breakdown and divorce often result, sometimes very rapidly.

7. Very often, one or both partners turn to outside sexual and emotional involvements, seeking what they lack in their marriage, or to prove that there is nothing wrong with them (meaning it's all their partner's fault!). For the aversive person, not uncommonly, sex with the new partner is enjoyed and looked forward to. However, should this new relationship progress to marriage, often aversion gradually develops all over again unless the predisposing, causative and perpetuating factors are overcome.

Types of Aversion

The commonest is the aversive man or woman who once enjoyed sex but no longer does (secondary aversion). Much less frequently seen is the person who has never liked it and always been aversive (primary aversion).

Primary aversion usually extends to include sexual contact with any and all partners, whereas secondary aversion is often confined to the spouse. Primary aversion is usually a much more difficult problem to overcome, and is very commonly associated with other major sexual dysfunctions.

What Causes Sexual Aversion?

Aversion is usually a complication of DSD, and therefore can be contributed to by all the factors which may produce this (see chapter 12). It tends to result when sex is repeatedly engaged in, despite an absence of interest, under conditions or circumstances where it is physically or emotionally unpleasant or painful. Faulty attitudes, not only about lovemaking and sex, predispose to it developing, and the problem progressively worsens as vicious circles are set up due to the individual's reactions to it, the partner's reactions to it, and defective communication between the couple about the problem.

Taking the most common situation of secondary aversion in a married woman, a very typical scenario goes something like this:

> She is overworked and chronically tired with too many responsibilities. This situation is often compounded by her possessing a rather perfectionistic attitude whereby she expects and demands too much of herself (and perhaps other family members). There is no time for herself and what she would really like to do. She puts the family first and is therefore often chronically unhappy and resentful. She has sex with her husband as a duty, when he wants it, despite the fact that almost none of her conditions are met. Not surprisingly, she gets little out of it, the more so because she doesn't have the key sexual attitude (chapter 10). She feels resentment when she sees her husband's pleasure and satisfaction, contrasting with what she experiences. Her interest in sex progressively decreases, and she increasingly finds sexual contact a frankly negative, frustrating emotional experience. However, she doesn't communicate with her husband about the problem and starts to avoid sexual contact as much as possible. Feeling rejected, he starts to put pressure on her for sex, causing her to feel even more resentful. She gets to the stage where she mainly has sex to relieve her escalating guilt, immediately afterwards feeling more resentment. Her husband starts to become angry, and arguments develop over sex, aggravating the problem and mauling the relationship.
>
> Note the general sequence:
>
> - loss of interest due to unfavorable conditions
> - continued sexual activity despite lack of interest, the wrong mental attitude to lovemaking, and unsatisfactory circumstances
> - increasingly unpleasant sexual experiences
> - failure of communication
> - negative emotional reactions by the woman to the whole situation
> - negative responses by the spouse
> - progressively increasing avoidance
> - progressively increasing negative reactions by both partners
> - deterioration in the couple's general relationship

The Sad Thing About Aversion

Aversion very often develops in a committed, basically sound relationship where fundamentally each partner loves the other. It often results from avoidable misunderstandings, faulty attitudes, poor communication, and defective problem solving. It may eventually destroy what is essentially a good marriage. Saddest of all, it is usually entirely preventable.

Personal Factors Associated With Aversion

Personality

Individuals who set themselves high standards, are prone to guilt and resentment, tend to bottle up dissatisfaction, and habitually put the needs of other family members ahead of their own, are especially vulnerable.

Faulty General Attitudes

1. **"Other people are responsible for my unhappiness."** The reality is that our unhappiness is usually very largely self-created, and that we must take personal responsibility for it!

2. **"Other people upset me by what they do and say."** The reality is that the only person who can upset you is yourself! You upset yourself over what other people do and say.

If what I have just stated seems hard to swallow, you will be convinced if you refer to one of the books on attitude change listed in appendix 4.

A Few Words on Secondary Aversion in the Male

The commonest situation is where, for various reasons, a man finds that sex with his partner has become not only boring but a real chore. For example, it takes too long to get her aroused, or to bring her to orgasm, or he can't bring her to orgasm at all (both erroneously believe he is responsible for her arousal and satisfaction). Or she always complains that he isn't doing it right, or that he ejaculates too quickly, or that he is guilty of some other deficiency. Whatever he does or doesn't do, she is unhappy about it. He gets increasingly little out of it himself and avoids sex, even when he occasionally feels like it, because it almost always means a tense protracted encounter, ending up with both partners uptight, dissatisfied, or frustrated. Impotence may result, and he then has an additional reason for avoidance—so he won't be confronted with his self-perceived sexual inadequacy. In this scenario, note once again the roles of faulty attitudes and defective communication, and how each partner's response to the difficulty ultimately compounds it.

Physical Factors Contributing to Aversion

If intercourse or orgasm or ejaculation are uncomfortable or painful due to a variety of gynecological problems in the woman or various urological disorders in the man, this can powerfully predispose to the development of aversion, for obvious reasons.

What You Can Do To Reverse Aversion

1. If intercourse or orgasm or ejaculation are physically uncomfortable or painful, you must consult with your doctor so that any medical problems can be recognized and dealt with.

2. You must work at developing the key sexual attitude (chapter 6 and session 1). Until you get this firmly established in your mind, you won't make much (or any) progress no matter what else you do!

3. You can work at not upsetting yourself, taking responsibility for your own happiness and pleasure, and modifying over-perfectionistic attitudes. Practical, self-help ways of doing this are described in the books by Ellis and Harper and by Lazarus and Fay listed in appendix 4.

4. You must improve the quality of your communication together.

5. You must negotiate with your partner mutually acceptable ways of handling all the various problem situations which repeatedly arise between you, both sexually and nonsexually. For example, as a first step to take the pressure off sex, you might agree to avoid all sexual contact for a specified period, during which time you will both make a special effort to have as much physical contact as you can (even if initially it feels uncomfortable) and to please each other as much as possible. Some of the practicalities of negotiation are described in chapter 17.

6. If relevant, you must try to modify an excessively busy, demanding, or stressful lifestyle so that your conditions can be reasonably approximated. What stress you simply can't avoid, you can, as it were, "neutralize" to a considerable degree by regular relaxation or meditation (sessions 6 and 7).

7. You will always use desensitization (session 8), first in imagination, then in the real-life situation, to overcome your automatic negative emotional reaction to sexual contact.

8. When the aversion has been reversed, you can profitably work on the underlying deficient sexual desire.

The Positive Side of Sexual Aversion

If often occurs in committed relationships that are basically sound in other areas. If both partners work hard at what has been suggested, it is usually not too difficult to reverse. A common end result of a succesful joint attack on sexual aversion is that the couple become much closer than ever before, i.e., their relationship is actually enhanced!

Chapter 15

Why Self-Help for Deficient Sexual Desire?

Problems of deficient sexual interest, with or without aversion to sexual contact, occur very commonly in both men and women. The effects can be far-reaching and severe, often adversely affecting marital happiness, self-esteem, and even such things as work performance. Sexual problems in many ways hit at people in the area in which they are most vulnerable.

There is little of worth on deficient sexual desire in the popular press, so that it is difficult for men and women to get accurate information on the problem. This unhappy situation is compounded by the fact that myths and misleading information on the problem and related issues abound and are widespread in the community.

From the medical and psychological point of view, defective sexual drive is often a most complex problem. Medical courses do not equip future medical practitioners to deal adequately with this, giving them only a basic idea of the issues involved and of the broad principles of treatment.

Even if the affected individual can overcome his or her anxiety and embarrassment to a degree sufficient to discuss the problem with a family doctor or other professional, it is not always easy to obtain referral to a specialist with all the necessary expertise, since there are few trained therapists specializing in the treatment of sexual disorders.

In spite of this, the fact remains that many cases of deficient sexual drive can be overcome using relatively simple treatment techniques. Modern sex therapy relies heavily on the prescription and performance of homework exercises, and the bulk of the treatment is actually done at home by the person himself or herself, under guidance.

If individuals afflicted with deficient sexual drive have a detailed, step-by-step description of what they must do to overcome their problem, then the need for consultation with a trained therapist can in many cases be overcome or greatly reduced.

It cannot be emphasized too strongly that a great deal can often be achieved using self-help procedures, provided they are fully understood and performed absolutely correctly. Over many years of clinical practice, I have developed a tremendous respect for a person's ability to help himself or herself and resolve problems using his or her own personal resources. All that a therapist contributes sometimes is a little guidance. In keeping with this experience, the aim of this portion of the book is to make readily available a wide range of self-help techniques so that men and women with problems of deficient libido can help themselves, almost as if they were being personally guided by an experienced therapist. There are, of course, situations in which medical investigation and treatment and specialized assistance are required, and these will be clearly indicated.

While this book is essentially directed at heterosexuals, the issues, principles, and techniques are equally relevant for, and applicable to, homosexuals.

Chapter 16

How To Evaluate a Problem of Deficient Sexual Desire and To Prepare for Self-management

Self-Evaluation

You must realize that there are important limitations on just how far you can go in working out the various factors contributing to your difficulty. This applies even if you have a good deal of medical and psychological knowledge, since we are all blind to many aspects of our particular situation because we are too close to it. Nonetheless, you can realistically aim to sort out some of the main issues and decide when you may need outside help.

Using the headings discussed in chapter 12 as a guide to the causes of deficient sexual drive, let us systematically check you out.

Chemical Factors

Are you exposed to any chemicals at work, socially, or in your hobbies? Are you taking any medications, prescribed or over-the-counter? If so, check them out as suggested in chapter 12.

It is worth knowing that caffeine (the stimulant drug in coffee, tea, and cola beverages) can make some people anxious and tense. If you drink these and feel they could be affecting you adversely, experiment to see whether stopping them completely makes you feel any better. If you try this, it may take a few months off all caffeine before you can decide if it is relevant, and you may feel miserable for about a week because of caffeine withdrawal effects.

If you often feel nervous or anxious and drink alcohol nearly every day or to excess, this may be contributing to the way you feel, even though the immediate effect of alcohol is temporarily to reduce anxiety. As a general rule, if you use alcohol regularly, even though it has no obvious ill effect, it is well worthwhile experimenting to see whether it is aggravating your problem by stopping completely for at least a month. If you find it difficult to stop drinking completely, you may have a drinking problem, and you should seek guidance as to whether you do, and if so, how you can overcome it. A good family physician will be able to help here.

Physical Contributions

These present a real problem in self-evaluation. There is no doubt that it would be desirable for you to have a full head-to-toes medical examination by your doctor. Because this is very time-consuming, you might have to arrange a special long appointment. Remember, however, that an "all-clear" finding from a competently performed general physical examination does not in any way mean there are no physical factors contributing to your problem. Some relevant disorders can only be recognized by special tests.

If you generally feel unwell or run down, if you have lost weight without dieting or have pain or lumps for which you do not already have a precise medical diagnosis, you need to be examined.

If you have noticed changes in your vision, sense of smell or hearing, or if you are aware of some loss of normal feeling or sensation, or of any weakness or clumsiness of the muscles in any part of your body, these must be medically assessed. Any unusual turns, headaches, or change in your speech should also be investigated.

Likewise, you should check out any recent change in the way you react to hot and cold weather, or have a tendency to drink more fluids and urinate more frequently.

Should you decide not to seek a general medical examination first-up because you feel well physically and have no symptoms other than DSD, you are probably not running much of a risk that some serious medical complaint is being missed. If, however, your problem fails to respond to the careful application of the self-help procedures to be described, I would *strongly* urge you to have a thorough general physical examination, even if you think you are perfectly healthy.

The guiding principles in evaluating yourself for possible physical contributions to deficient sexual drive must be crystal clear to you! To recap, they are listed below.

1. Ideally, you would have a full general physical examination.
2. If you have any physical symptoms or abnormalities, particularly the ones detailed above, see your doctor. If so, while you are there you might as well also ask to be given a thorough general physical examination.
3. If you feel completely well and have no symptoms other than deficient libido, you will probably come to no harm if you choose not to have a general physical examination first-up. However, if your problem does not respond to the measures outlined in this book, you should then have a full physical examination no matter how well you feel.

Always remember the other side of the medical situation—no abnormalities found on general physical examination and the complete absence of physical symptoms do not in any way guarantee that there are no physical factors contributing to your deficient libido.

A note on the possible relevance of chemical and physical factors in cases of situational DSD. If your problem of DSD is clearly situational, in that you have a perfectly normal interest in sexual activity in one situation but not in another, logic would appear to dictate that chemical and physical contributory factors simply can't be relevant in your case. While this is very likely to be true, there can be exceptions, since one's brain can override the effects of physical contributions under some circumstances. With this in mind, it is probably best to *play safe* and follow the suggestions I have offered above. At least they can do you no harm!

Psychological Contributions

For convenience, these have been divided into personal and relationship issues.

Personal Factors

Psychological Stress

Have a good look at your life circumstances and see if you operate under too much stress or pressure. If you do, what can be done to minimize it? What stresses you can't avoid, you can to some extent "neutralize" by the regular practice of some formal relaxation procedure. See sessions 6 and 7.

Psychiatric Illness

It is vitally important to check out the possibility that you have what is technically known as a "depressive illness," which is a very common ailment. This is quite a complex issue medically, especially since you can have this without really feeling depressed. If you often feel down, gloomy, guilty, don't like yourself, wonder whether life is really worth living, don't sleep very well, have little interest in things that you previously enjoyed, find that you have to really push yourself to perform many ordinary tasks, feel tense, anxious, irritable, don't really enjoy your food as you previously did, lack energy or get tired very easily, have lost weight, can't concentrate or find your memory is not good, then you may very well have a depressive illness. Of course, nobody with this disorder has *all* these complaints. If you have some of them, even if you don't feel particularly depressed, check it out with a doctor. Having a depressive illness is actually good news, because often it is relatively easy to treat, and when you are over it, your libido may be restored without doing anything else.

Unrealistic Expectations

Have you and your partner worked out and written down your list of conditions for being sexually interested and responsive? Are you reading these lists every day, as suggested in chapter 7?

Have you worked at laying to rest those sexual myths affecting you, discussed in chapter 6? Have you really developed the key sexual attitude (chapter 6) so that it is automatic and has replaced your old destructive attitudes? If you haven't already done these things, do yourself a big favor and do them now before you move on any further!

Poor Self-Image

Sit back and think about yourself. Do you really like yourself as a person? Are you reasonably satisfied with yourself? Are you acceptably confident? Do you feel reasonably comfortable with your physical appearance? How would your partner answer these questions about you? Do you think these factors in any way adversely influence your sexual behavior? If so, write down all the practical ways in which they affect your interest in sex. See if you can discuss these with your partner.

Should you feel you need to do something about your self-image, try the approaches directed at this problem described in Ellis and Harper's book on rational thinking (see appendix 4).

Sexual Boredom

Think about a typical sexual encounter with your partner. Is there a sameness about it? Has it become pretty dull? Write down your own contributions to this state of affairs, and ask your partner to do the same. Then discuss your own deficiencies with each other. Be constructive and avoid any criticism of each other. See if you can come up with some practical suggestions to improve things in this area and write them down. I have offered some suggestions for avoiding and overcoming this problem in chapter 18.

Ungratifying Sexual Experiences

Think about your average sexual encounter with your partner and write down anything which happens or doesn't happen that for you stops it from being as enjoyable as it could be. Ask your partner to do the same. Then, bending over backwards not to be critical, gently discuss your lists together. Be constructive, not negative. See if you can come up with some mutually agreed upon positive suggestions to make lovemaking more fulfilling. Write these down and do your respective bests to enact these when you do make love.

Performance Anxiety

Look at the kinds of thoughts you tend to have *before, during, and after* lovemaking. Do you think about your sexual performance or about what your partner will think of it? If so, amongst other things, you still have a way to go in making the key sexual attitude (chapter 6) truly yours! Keep hammering away at the relevant "doing" exercises (chapter 6 and session 1).

Excessive Concern With Pleasing Your Partner

Reflect on a typical sexual encounter with your partner and see if this applies to you. What does your partner think? If this seems to be an issue, reread with your partner the section on sexual rights and responsibilities (chapter 7) and discuss it together. Then discuss with him or her what you can both do during lovemaking to overcome this problem. Write down your agreed upon final list of practical suggestions and do your respective bests to enact them when you do make love.

Active Trying

Are you ever aware that you actively try to force yourself to become interested or aroused? What does your partner think? Does he or she ever actually really try to make you respond? Agree to remind each other gently of this error should either of you become aware of it in yourself or in your partner.

Anxiety and Guilt About Sex and Pleasure

Think over a recent sexual encounter with your partner and/or a recent episode of masturbation. Were you aware at any stage, before, during, or after, of any feelings of anxiety or guilt? What does your partner think? If the answer is yes, do the following:

1. Write down all the events from your remembered past that might possibly have caused you to associate sex with anxiety or guilt. Talk them over with your partner if you can.
2. Work out the kinds of thoughts you tend to have before, during, or after lovemaking that cause you to feel anxious or guilty. To do this, you may have to replay a recent encounter in your mind with your eyes closed, or pay attention to your thoughts the next time you make love. Write down what these destructive thoughts are. They will be used later on.

Fear of Venereal Disease
If this is a realistic issue, for example, because your partner periodically has genital herpes, the pair of you should seek informed medical advice. If you realize that your fear is irrational, try to talk it over with your partner, emphasizing how unreasonable it is. You might then try to overcome it by a rational thinking approach, using the book by Ellis and Harper listed in appendix 4. It this doesn't help, you will probably need professional assistance. Simple do-it-yourself desensitization (session 8) usually doesn't work with venereophobia.

Fear of Unwanted Pregnancy
If this is a realistic problem, you *must* discuss the issue of effective contraception with your partner. You may both need to get informed medical advice. If you know that your fear is irrational, try a rational thinking approach, using Ellis and Harper's book. Desensitization (session 8) is also worth trying.

Fear of Having a Heart Attack
If this is an issue, first get specific advice from a specialist cardiologist. If despite this you are still concerned about this possibility, try a rational thinking approach, using Ellis and Harper's book listed in appendix 4. If that doesn't help, you will need professional assistance.

Specific Traumatic Events
If you know that some particular trauma has interfered with your ability to enjoy yourself sexually, this will have to be "laid to rest." As a first step, see if you can discuss your feelings with your partner about what happened. However, be very careful doing this if the trauma was inflicted by your partner. Other measures will be described in the next chapter.

Irrational Dangers and Sexual Phobias
Write down *anything* to do with sex about which you are in any way anxious. Don't confine yourself just to lovemaking and its options, but cover having sexual thoughts and fantasies, masturbating, feeling aroused, initiating or declining lovemaking, and so on. See if you can discuss these with your partner and ask if he or she can add to your list. This information will be used later in your treatment and is very important.

Nonspecific Dysphoria (Negative Mood)
Think about the way you often feel. Do you frequently feel angry, resentful, anxious, tense, guilty, and so on? If so, see if you can work out and write down what causes you to feel like this. Discuss what you have come up with with your partner, being very careful not to be seen as either critical or complaining. Can he or she see reasons you can't? See if you can together work out what you can do to overcome this dysphoria. Very often the best remedy will be to correct faulty ways of thinking, as described in the books on attitude change listed in appendix 4.

Irrational Anger
Evaluate and deal with this, as discussed above under the heading "Anxiety and Guilt About Sex and Pleasure."

The Automatic Turnoff Mechanism
Be very honest and thorough evaluating yourself for this! Put your mental microscope over a recent sexual opportunity or encounter, and see if you can work out the kinds of thoughts you tend to have when sex is a possibility or an actuality. Write them down. The next time you have a sexual opportunity, take note of the thoughts you find yourself having and add them to your list, which will be used later on. For the moment, see if you can discuss it with your partner.

Distrust
If when you reflect on yourself you feel that lack of, or difficulty with, trust is a significant issue for you in any area of your relationship, not just the sexual one, do the following. First read what I have said about trust in session 18. Then write down all the experiences you can recall from your past that may have caused you to lack trust. See if you can discuss them with your partner, being *extremely* gentle and noncritical if some of these have applied to him or her. If lack of trust is contributing to your DSD, these events will have to be laid to rest emotionally, so keep your list for future reference.

Fear of Intimacy and Commitment
Reflect on your significant relationships with partners over the years and see if you can see any evidence of the pattern described under this heading in chapter 12. Talk the general issue over with your partner and see if this may be relevant in your relationship. If so, write down all the things you can think of from your past that could have made you uneasy about closeness and commitment and see if you can discuss these in detail with your partner. Also discuss what I have said about intimacy in session 18.

Sexual Dysfunction
If either of you have other difficulties affecting your sexual enjoyment or function, sit down and discuss these together, being very careful not to be seen as critical or complaining! See if you can decide what relationship these other problems have to your DSD. Decide together whether anything needs to be done about these problems, and if so, how and when. Appendix 1 may be useful here.

Infertility
If this is a problem, it is *crucially* important that you together talk over your respective feelings about the situation. If you actually have an insoluble solution but it still distresses you, you may get help from a rational thinking approach, as described in Ellis and Harper's book listed in appendix 4.

Relationship Factors

Let me warn you in advance that it is very difficult to self-evaluate objectively and accurately for relationship contributions to your deficient sexual drive. That should not stop you from trying, preferably with the help of your partner, but do not be surprised if you don't get very far. Remember my rules of thumb:

1. Your partner's responses to your sexual problems often, if not usually, inadvertently make them worse, even in the very best relationships.
2. Your prospects for overcoming your sexual difficulty with your partner hinge on the true quality of your relationship with him or her.

Check out the following possibilities, being as truthful as you can.

Lack of Knowledge About Proper Erotic Technique

A lot of otherwise intelligent people believe that lovemaking ability comes naturally without the need for any special information. If either you or your partner have never thoroughly read a book on lovemaking techniques, preferably one published in the last 10 years, you can assume that there are deficiencies in your knowledge. The remedy is simple and obvious.

Partner Adherence to Behavior Controlled by Sexual Myths

By now, hopefully, you have both read chapter 6 and have both done what I have suggested to overcome the destructive effects of those myths that have adversely affected your sexual relationship. If you haven't, do yourself a big favor and go no further until you both have. If you find some of these myths hard to overcome, try some of the additional techniques suggested in session 4.

Mismatched Libidos

If this is relevant in your case, make sure you have both read and together thoroughly discussed chapter 10. If my suggestions for handling your situation aren't right for you, together negotiate a mutually acceptable compromise. Make sure you then write it down.

Lack of Loving Feelings Toward Your Partner

If this is a problem in your case, it may help to remember that you don't love a person, you love their behavior (for example, what they do and say). If your partner can be induced to change some of his or her behaviors in line with your expectations, it may well be that loving feelings will reemerge. Of course, you can't make yourself love a person, and some relationships have passed the point of no return. When you are feeling negative toward your partner (i.e., unloving), it can sometimes be helpful to say to yourself something like this: "OK, so I feel negative toward (him, her) now, but really its only (his, her) behavior that I dislike; basically I care for (him, her) as a person."

Some couple procedures for negotiating more desirable behaviors in each other will be discussed in the next section.

Marital Conflict

If you feel there are significant problems in the nonsexual aspects of your relationship, it is *extremely important* to try to overcome these before directly tackling the problem of DSD. If things haven't deteriorated too far, you may be able to help yourselves by sitting down and talking about your differences, always trying to negotiate mutually acceptable compromises. In the next chapter, I will describe a simple and effective way of doing this. To follow it, you will both need first to spend some time alone, providing detailed and thoughtful answers to the following questions.

1. What are all the things my partner says or does that please me? Remember to include all the little things we so often take for granted, such as "is punctual," "dresses neatly," and so on. Try to avoid generalizations, such as "is caring"—translate such a broad statement into many separate, more specific examples: "takes over the ironing when I'm tired," "opens the car door for me," "doesn't bother me with her problems when I'm uptight," and so on.
2. What are all the things my partner says or does that displease me? Include all the little annoyances, even if they seem very trivial (e.g., "squeezes the toothpaste in the middle instead of at the bottom"). Remember, try to avoid generalizations.

Do not discuss these lists with your partner until you have read how to do it optimally in the next chapter.

If (or when) it is obvious that your relationship problems are beyond your ability to resolve alone, seek out a professional counsellor.

Unrealistic and Therefore Unmet Expectations

If, after reading the section on this in chapter 12, you feel this could be a relevant issue in your case, both of you should spend some time alone, providing detailed and thoughtful answers to all the following questions.

1. In a perfect marriage, what would a man do? What would a woman do? What would a man not do? What would a woman not do?
2. In our marriage, I think the man should do the following things and not do the following things. I think the woman should do the following things and not do the following things.
3. In a perfect sexual relationship, what would a man do? What would a woman do? What would a man not do? What would a woman not do?
4. In the sexual side of our marriage, I think the man should do the following things and not do the following things. I think the woman should do the following things and not do the following things.

Now answer questions 1 to 4 above, all over again, pretending that you are your partner.

Having done all this, sit down with your partner and, over a number of sessions, discuss all your lists, taking the questions in the above order, alternating with one item from each other's lists. Begin with the lists you wrote pretending you were your partner. You should not get into a hassle over this if you remember that there are no right or wrong answers, only opinions, and that all of us have an absolute right to our own opinion on anything, even if it is stupid! Most couples, even those without any overt problems, find this a very revealing exercise. It almost always highlights how little you have ever communicated some very basic and important issues.

This exercise should help you clear the air and enable you to negotiate mutually acceptable compromises. Remember, all successful relationships are based on fairly hefty mutual compromises.

Failure To Communicate Sexual and Emotional Needs

Read with your partner what I have written on this in chapter 12. If you both agree you have a problem in this area, start doing the sexual communication exercise (session 16) together.

Perceived Nonsexual Uses of Sex

Try to be *painfully honest* with yourself, and see if, at least occasionally, you engage in sex for reasons that have nothing to do with a sexual need or appetite. Write down what you come up with. Ask your partner to do the same thing. Now gently discuss these lists together, bending over backwards not to be critical or hurtful! A good opening line to defuse this (often painful) discussion is something like this: "Until I sat down and really thought about it, I simply never realized . . . "

Childish Expectations

If this is causing problems in your relationship, you should have thrashed the issues out in the exercises I gave you to do under the heading "Unrealistic and Therefore Unmet Expectations." If you have not already done so, do them now!

Inappropriate Partner Responses to Sexual Problems

Since this is virtually always relevant, you should do the following. Write down all the things you can think of that your partner has said or done (or not said, or not done) when you haven't been interested in, or responsive during, sex. Has he or she ever

- been angry?
- looked angry, but said nothing?
- gone silent?
- sulked?
- tried to pressure you?
- nagged you?

- tried to make you feel guilty?
- blamed you?
- punished you?
- been unaffectionate?
- threatened you?
- done anything else unhelpful?

All these responses, unfortunately, usually make DSD (or any other sexual problem) worse.

Get your partner to do the same exercise, writing down his or her perception of how he or she has behaved when you weren't interested in, or responsive during, sex. Gently discuss together what you have come up with. Since this exercise has a high potential for hurt feelings and conflict, bend over backwards not to be critical! It helps if you emphasize that what you have written is just your opinion, or your perception, or your memory, and that you could be in error.

When you have done this, see if together you can work out a number of more appropriate responses that will help, not hinder. Write them down for future reference.

A Note for Individuals Without a Current Partner

Obviously, many of the "things to do" in this chapter can't be performed without a partner. Do whatever you can alone, and answer the questions about relationships as they applied in past involvements.

Preparing for Direct Treatment

It is important to start the direct attack on your problem with as much going for you as possible. With this philosophy in mind, before you move on to the exercises specifically directed at regaining your libido, first attend to the following:

1. Do what you can about any drug or chemical factors that may be contributing to your problem, including alcohol and caffeine.
2. If indicated, check out with your doctor any possible physical contributions to your difficulty and get any necessary medical treatment.
3. Minimize any stresses, and work to overcome the adverse effects of stress by regular formal relaxation (sessions 6 and 7).
4. If you could have a depressive illness, seek medical advice and treatment.
5. Make sure you have your own, and your partner's, final lists of conditions (chapter 7). Read both every day.

6. Make sure you have dealt with any myths adversely affecting your sexual expression (chapter 6 and possibly session 4). Read your lists of new, more rational attitudes every day.
7. Make sure you have truly developed the key sexual attitude (chapter 6 and appendix 1).
8. Make sure you have thoroughly worked through all the relevant suggestions for things to do, described in this chapter.

If applicable in your case, you will have the following lists for use in the next chapter:

1. All the events from your past which might have caused you to associate sex with anxiety, or guilt, or anger.
2. All the kinds of thoughts you tend to have before, during, and after lovemaking, which are not helpful because they make you feel anxious, guilty, or angry, and they constitute the "automatic turnoff mechanism."
3. A list of relevant past traumatic events (if any).
4. A list of anything to do with sex about which you are in any way anxious.
5. A list of past events that have caused you to have trust problems.
6. A list of all the things your partner says or does that please you (both partners' lists).
7. A list of all the things your partner says or does that displease you (both partners' lists).

Chapter 17

A Self-Help Program for Deficient Sexual Desire

The process of overcoming your problem of deficient sexual drive and gaining confidence in your sexual capacity revolves around homework exercises and a number of interlocking "requirements." The more of these requirements that can be properly met, the better your outlook for success.

Requirement 1
You must accept the fact that it will probably take some considerable time to overcome your problem.

Requirement 2
If you have a partner, you must communicate about your problem openly and honestly.

Requirement 3
You must practice what is required regularly, thoroughly, and under reasonably good conditions.

Requirement 4
You must have the correct mental attitude to sexual expression.

Requirement 5
You must do what you can to make sure that your conditions for being sexually interested and responsive are adequately met as often as possible.

How Long Will It Take?

This will, of course, depend on many factors. The important rules are:

1. Make haste slowly.
2. Go at your own comfortable pace.
3. Do not move from one step to the next until you have thoroughly mastered the present one.

Under good conditions, where everything goes more or less according to plan, it will probably take you at least three months to master what needs to be done. It may take much longer, largely depending on how much time you have available to practice. You can't make your problem disappear, you can only allow it to go away! It is better to move along slowly and steadily and get there in the end, than to rush and perhaps miss out on success.

What About Your Partner?

A truly caring and cooperative partner is your greatest asset in overcoming your problem. However, if he or she is to help you maximally, he or she must understand as much as possible about your problem, and *especially* how you feel about it. You will certainly find that sharing your anxieties, shame, guilt, anger, and so on will make you feel much better, and take a lot of psychological pressure off your shoulders, and even more importantly off your sexual functioning.

How To Get the Most From the Exercises

You will find there are a variety of exercises for you to master and perform. As a general rule, a little done frequently tends to be more effective than a large amount done occasionally. Try to arrange your daily/weekly schedule so that you can spend on average 30 to 60 minutes of *prime time* each day, working at various aspects of what has to be done. Prime time means when you are alert, able to concentrate fully, and feel reasonably good. By and large, it is a waste of time to try to force yourself to practice your exercises under poor conditions, for example, when you are in a hurry, uptight, tired, and so on. You may have to have a long, hard look at your routine and your priorities to permit the necessary practice under really good conditions, and you will probably have to ruthlessly prune off a few nonessential activities or chores! However, if you really wish to succeed, you will somehow find enough regular prime time *whatever the difficulties* that have to be overcome to achieve this! All exercises must be performed exactly as described and very thoroughly.

What Is the Correct Mental Attitude?

Lovemaking means literally that—interacting physically and emotionally with someone you care for. Arousal, intercourse, and orgasm are merely nonessential options.

As thus defined, lovemaking can *never* be a failure. Whatever happens, it can only be a success.

If you have done what I have suggested to date and resisted the temptation to go too fast, this attitude should now be firmly entrenched. If it isn't, hammer away at developing it, as suggested, before going any further.

Working at Having Your "Conditions" Met

Hopefully by now you will be reading your lists of conditions for being sexually interested and responsive every morning! Naturally you will also do whatever you can about yourself and your overall environment to have as many of these met as often as is humanly possible! You will, for example, try to avoid fatigue, eliminate or minimize physical discomfort, avoid making yourself uptight, maximize the good things in your relationship with your partner, and so on, as worked out in chapter 7.

Your Exercise Plan

I am assuming that by now you have done everything relevant that I suggested in the last chapter and, in particular, what I summarized at the end of it. If you haven't, go back and do it before you go any further.

The next step is to negotiate a *formal agreement* with your partner about how you will both handle sex while you are working to overcome your problem of DSD. What you are aiming for is to defuse the sexual situation and take all pressure off performance. Basically, you have two options:

1. You can use the handling techniques for managing mismatched libidos described in chapter 10. These will involve you in some personal sexual contact with your partner, but with absolutely no pressure to perform and no adverse reactions if you don't.

2. If you don't think that at this stage you could handle the suggestions in chapter 10, then you will both have to agree to avoid all sexual contact together for a specified time. At the end of that time, you will together reconsider the situation in the light of your progress in the treatment program and negotiate a new formal agreement.

Now work out and write down the approximate times each day when you are going to practice your exercises. Remember, you need prime time, and if you are really motivated to succeed, you will somehow find the time whatever the practical difficulties!

Next, select those exercises from the lists below which are essential, and those which seem relevant to your particular situation. If in doubt as to whether you need to do a particular exercise, *do it anyway*. It is better to play safe and have as much going for you as possible.

Keep an appropriately ruled notebook in which you put a tick every time you do each specific exercise. You will have the days of the week going across the page and the names of the exercises going down the page. Leave it open, in some place where you will see it often, such as on your dressing table or desk. The idea is to remind you, motivate you, and keep you honest! You will find you have a tendency to do the things you enjoy and avoid the exercises you don't particularly like (which are usually the most important). If you do fall into this trap, this fact will be clearly apparent from your exercise notebook.

Summary of the Basic Treatment

As you can now see, this involves the following:

1. Getting your attitudes right
2. Getting your circumstances right
3. Taking the pressure off sexual performance
4. Exercises to overcome factors inhibiting sexual desire
5. Exercises to promote and stimulate sexual desire

What now follows relates to items 4 and 5.

Exercises You Do Alone

Let's consider first what you will do without your partner.

Thought stopping. Master this if any kind of unhelpful thoughts tend to come into your mind when sex is a possibility, or during or after sexual contact.

Coping self-statements. If you are "uptight" (anxious, angry, guilty, etc.) during or in anticipation of sexual contact, master this simple technique and see if you find it helpful.

The "observer" technique. If you tend to have unhelpful thoughts (and associated feelings) during or in anticipation of sexual contact, and if thought stopping doesn't seem to be the answer for you (after a fair trial), try this technique.

Talking sense to the unconscious. If you tend to have unhelpful thoughts (and associated feelings) during or in anticipation of sexual contact, particularly if these are clearly related to past experiences, and if thought stopping and the observer technique just don't seem right for you, you might master and try this procedure.

Autosuggestion. Apart from any previous use you might have already made of this simple technique, to change faulty attitudes based on myths you can now use it to help break away from the adverse effects of some remembered past traumatic event, should this be relevant in your case. Suggest to yourself that the past is the past and that you will no longer allow the event to spoil your love life.

Self-monitoring. You should always do this. Keep going until your problem is ancient history.

Self-relaxation. Master one of the two techniques described if

a. You are uptight (anxious, angry, guilty, etc.) during or in anticipation of sexual contact.
b. Your life is stressful.
c. You need to use desensitization.

Meditation. Master this if

a. You need to relax, but find that neither of the two techniques described above relaxes your mind (as opposed to your body).
b. You find it difficult to keep unhelpful thoughts out of your mind despite the measures described above.
c. You find it hard to concentrate on the sensual, erotic aspects of the experience during lovemaking (or masturbation).

Desensitization. The *imaginal technique* should be used for the following purposes:

1. To get rid of anxiety (or anger or guilt, etc.) about any aspect of normal sexual behavior, including (if relevant) feeling sexual desire, having sexual thoughts, fantasizing, masturbating, and every facet of normal lovemaking.

The data needed before you can proceed involves working out a series of scenarios, exactly as described in session 8, covering prototypical past, and possible future, sexual situations. Include scenes covering even sexual behavior that you can't see yourself ever being involved in, even though you know intellectually that it is perfectly normal.

2. To neutralize, or lay to rest, past traumas or events which could or have caused you to associate sex with anxiety, guilt, or anger, or which have caused trust problems.

Use the lists of past, possibly relevant events developed in the last chapter. Take each event and break it up into a number of scenarios that capture the highlights (perhaps more appropriately, the lowlights) of the trauma.

For example, if your mother caught you masturbating as a child or adolescent and severely punished you for it, you might break this event down into the following scenarios.

1. "I am 14. I am masturbating, lying on my bed. Mom has just

walked in and caught me."

2. "I am 14. Mom is abusing me for masturbating, telling me it is a filthy, evil habit, and that it will soften my brain and make me into an imbecile."
3. "I am 14. Mom has just told Dad I was masturbating earlier that day. He is giving me a tongue lashing over it."
4. I am 14. Mom is checking my sheets to see if I have been masturbating."

If you can't recall the event in such detail, imagine what possibly happened and write this down. Try to cover each event comprehensively, i.e., what led up to it, the event itself, and the worst of the aftermath. For really ugly traumas, you might have as many as 15 scenarios, occasionally even more. If a trauma was repeatedly inflicted, for example, if an older brother repeatedly forced you to have sex with him when you were a child, use only a single prototypical sequence of events.

If you have been unfortunate enough to have numerous traumatic events in your background, you may wind up with a lot of scenes. However, you have no choice but to lay the past to rest, and it involves as much work as it takes. In my practice, a few patients have had nearly 100 scenes to work through in this manner.

Real-life Desensitization. If, after finishing imaginal desensitization, you still feel somewhat uneasy about actual sexual behavior, then take the desensitization technique one step further, into real life, as described in session 8.

Elaborated writing. Use this to assist in "neutralizing," or laying to rest, one or several major traumatic events from your past if, after you have done your best to do this with desensitization, thoughts and memories of the incident(s) still upset you.

Pelvic muscle exercise. You should always do this.

Sensuality training exercises. You should always do these. They are crucially important to success.

Fantasy exercises. You should always do these.

Guided imagery. Unless you don't have access to a tape recorder, you should always do this. Even if you can't use a tape, it is still useful for both you and your partner to write out your descriptions of ideal lovemaking, so that you can both read them and see what would be perfect for each other.

Individual stimulation exercises. You should always do these. If you feel too anxious or uncomfortable about this, you might first have to use imaginal desensitization to overcome this problem.

Note: You can tackle the various individual exercises in any order you find most appropriate, although obviously some must be mastered before you can do others or know whether others are really necessary. Don't forget to keep a written daily record of what you do.

Exercises You Can Do With Your Partner

A few individual exercises may ultimately involve some partner participation, for example, real-life desensitization, guided imagery, and perhaps some of the fantasy exercises. Involve him or her in these only when you feel good and ready.

Sexual vocabulary exercise. You should always do this. Start whenever you feel like it.

Sexual communication exercise. You should probably always do this, even if you think you have no actual communication problem. You can start this whenever you like, and *the sooner the better!*

Shared sensuality exercises. You must always do these. Begin whenever you feel you would be reasonably comfortable with the earliest steps.

Exercises to develop trust and emotional closeness. Should you feel you have a problem in this area or a need for greater trust or closeness together, read what I have said about the issues in session 18. Then begin working on the things you can do, both by yourself and together, whenever you feel like it.

Shared stimulation exercises. You should always do these, but not until you have achieved all the goals of both parts of the shared sensuality exercises

Negotiating mutually desired behaviors. You can start this whenever you like. If there are obvious relationship problems, do it sooner rather than later.

Sit down with your partner and, over a number of sessions, work through both your lists of pleasing and displeasing behaviors (chapter 16) in the following way, alternating.

Read a pleasing behavior to your partner, then elaborate on it. Then read a displeasing one and elaborate on that. While you are doing this, your partner should listen carefully but say absolutely nothing! When you have finished, he or she should only summarize your expressed dissatisfaction, aloud, to check that it is clearly understood. Then you ask him or her what (if anything) he or she would be prepared to do to try to change this particular behavior just to please you. After discussing his or her best offer, write it down! Don't make yourself hurt or upset about occasional refusals.

Note that neither of you makes any attempt to justify your expressed dissatisfaction, or to prove to the other that they are wrong. Issues of right and wrong are totally irrelevant in this context! We are dealing only with opinions and preferences, and each of you has an inalienable, absolute right to have your own opinions and preferences. If you adhere *rigidly* to the above ground rules for this exercise, you simply cannot get into an argument.

Note carefully that agreeing to change some aspect of your behavior to please your partner is not in any way an admission that you were wrong.

You are merely agreeing to try to behave in a manner more pleasing to your partner, simply because you care about them. This is just part of the inevitable, numerous compromises we all have to make to be happy in our relationship.

Note also that neither of you is promising anything other than to do your best to do certain things and not to do certain other things simply to please your partner.

You will finish up with two lists, one for each of you, describing what you have agreed to try to do (or not do) to please your partner. Read both lists every day, preferably in the morning. You do this to remind yourself what you have to try to do and what your partner is trying to do. You need to remind yourself what he or she is attempting so that you can compliment your partner in some way every time you see an effort being made to please you. If you don't reinforce these efforts with praise and appreciation, they will soon cease!

When you observe that your partner has failed to do (or not do) something he or she has undertaken to try to change, say absolutely nothing and pretend you didn't notice. Just carry on as if it hadn't happened! Almost anything you could say runs the risk of making the undesired behavior occur more often, so belt up! *Note:* Saying nothing does not mean going silent; this also will merely tend to make things worse. Saying nothing means carrying on normally as if nothing undesirable had happened.

Don't forget to keep a written daily record of the various joint exercises as you do them.

Obviously, if you do not have a partner with whom you can perform the shared exercises, these cannot be done. While this makes your task more difficult, it certainly does not mean that you can't overcome your problem! In this situation, put all your efforts into the individual exercises and really make them count. Also, carefully study and think about the suggestions for lovemaking with a new partner. See chapter 18 and session 22.

If you have a steady partner but he or she won't cooperate in the treatment program, you have relationship problems, or he or she has personal sexual difficulties or both. This situation is best dealt with by seeking the assistance of a professional.

What To Do If You Don't Get Results

First reread the book from the beginning with your partner. Make sure you have fully understood *everything* and, most particularly, done *everything* I have asked you to do absolutely thoroughly. Redo carefully anything you realize you have too quickly glossed over.

Next, if this first manuever doesn't do the trick, the time has come for professional assessment and help. Your family doctor would be the first port of call. He or she can evaluate for possible physical contributions and determine who would be the most appropriate professional to refer you to.

Now read the final chapter before commencing your direct attack on your problem of DSD.

Chapter 18

Special Issues

Pregnancy

As a general rule, there is no reason why a couple cannot continue to enjoy their sexual relationship right throughout a normal pregnancy. Some uncommon obstetrical problems make actual intercourse undesirable or unsafe, but as explained previously, a couple certainly don't have to have intercourse to make love and be sexually fulfilled.

The most common libidinal response of women to their pregnancy is a gradual, progressive decrease in sexual drive or interest throughout pregnancy. However, some women report that pregnancy has no effect whatsoever on their sexual interest, and some find their libido considerably increased, at least for a period.

Pregnancy can also affect a man's libido: sometimes it increases, sometimes it decreases, while most usually it is unaffected. Some men completely lose their sexual interest in their wife when she becomes pregnant or after delivery. This situation is sometimes referred to as the "Madonna Syndrome." The notion here is that once his partner becomes pregnant, she is regarded as a mother and not a sexual partner. Not his own mother, of course, but the cherished mother of his infant. The man is typically tender, caring, and concerned toward his wife, but his erotic feelings are suppressed or directed elsewhere.

Misconceptions about alleged harmful effects of sexual activity during pregnancy are widespread, in both men and women, and can powerfully influence sexual drive. Inappropriate and unnecessary sexual abstinence or refusal during pregnancy can have damaging effects on a marriage. It is one cause of a man becoming involved in an affair during the pregnancy, and the effects of this on his marriage can be very destructive, even if it remains undiscovered.

In those few pregnancies where an obstetrician advises the woman against intercourse, or even orgasm, there are, of course, other fulfilling sexual options. Discrepancies in sexual drive during pregnancy should be handled as discussed in chapter 10.

Whatever pregnancy itself does to a woman's libido, it often decreases or is absent for a few months after delivery. There are many possible reasons for this, but fatigue, interrupted sleep, and a preoccupation with the care and welfare of the baby are often the most important. Additionally, intercourse may be uncomfortable or painful for a time for physical reasons, and this tends, of course, to decrease interest in sexual activity. Uncaring or selfish partner pressure for sex often further aggravates the situation, generating a vicious circle of progressively decreasing sexual interest. Occasionally the woman develops a chronic lack of interest in sex, or even aversion to sexual contact, as a result of this mismanagement of an understandable and normally temporary situation.

Prevention of pregnancy-related difficulties lies in open discussion of the problems and a mutual commitment to the best possible compromise until the situation rights itself.

Sexual Monotony

No matter how much a couple love each other and find their partner sexually attractive, it is easy to slip into the trap of sexual monotony, discussed in chapter 12. This can lead to a decrease in, or loss of, sexual interest, at least for one's partner! Avoiding this unhappy situation is an ongoing problem for all caring couples.

The best preventative is for both partners to be constantly aware of the need for variety and change. What about lovemaking in a different place, such as out of doors or on the lounge room floor? What about occasional careful preparation for luxurious lovemaking, in much the same way as one plans and prepares for a special dinner party? What about trying something different? Reading together an exposition on lovemaking techniques should give you plenty of ideas! Agreeing to alternate taking responsibility for at least some minor change each time you make love is another very good tip. Sometimes reading mutually appropriate erotic material together helps to break the chain of utter predictability.

There is a trap to be avoided here, and that is going to the other extreme of compulsive variety! Some people become so preoccupied with making things different that this becomes an end in itself, rather than a means to an end. *Never lose sight of the real goal of lovemaking,* which is for both of you to enjoy a very special, close physical and emotional encounter.

Non-monogamous Desires

A common concern of many absolutely normal people is that while they love their partner and enjoy sex with him or her, they also find themselves sexually attracted to, or interested in, other individuals. This may cause them to feel very guilty, that they are "oversexed," that they don't really love their partner, or that they are at dire risk of actually becoming sexually involved with someone else.

The facts are that *most* normal people, *occasionally* or even often, find themselves sexually attracted to other people, or thinking about sex with someone else. This is perfectly normal. This, of course, is not to say that someone who never experiences any sexual interest toward somebody other than their partner has a problem, as this situation is also perfectly normal, there being a very wide range to normal behavior.

The practical issue is not, "Is it normal or not?" but "What am I going to do about it?" We all have the ability to control our behavior under ordinary circumstances, and we will not act on our non-monogamous desires unless we make a deliberate conscious decision to do so. Quite apart from moral issues, the decision to act or not to act on these desires will, one would hope, be influenced by a mature analysis of the likely cost/benefit prospects.

Sexual Phobias

These have been discussed to some extent in chapter 12. Remember, a phobia is a persistent, irrational fear of something, associated with avoidance of whatever is feared.

It is important to understand that phobic anxiety has two components: "anticipatory" anxiety and "exposure" anxiety. Anticipatory anxiety is experienced in the absence of the phobic stimulus, merely because of the possibility (however remote) that exposure might occur. With many phobias, the anticipatory anxiety is the main or only source of discomfort, as exposure rarely or never occurs. Anticipatory anxiety with a sexual phobia might involve, for example, increasing tension and apprehension around the time a spouse is due home, because of the possibilty of anxiety-provoking sexual contact later in the evening, no matter how unlikely that may be.

Sometimes sexual phobias are associated with panic attacks, i.e., in anticipation of, or when confronted with, the specific sexual situation irrationally feared, panic episodes are induced. There is a sudden onset of intense apprehension or terror, sometimes associated with a feeling of impending doom. There may be associated breathlessness, palpitations, sweating, shaking, choking or smothering sensations, pins and needles, dizziness, giddiness, feelings of unreality, and chest pain or discomfort.

If such panic attacks are present, they indicate the need for professional assistance, which might well include the prescription of specific anti-panic medication.

Sometimes the social consequences of sexual phobias are extreme. Some afflicted individuals may avoid all contact with potential sex partners, remaining virginal, celibate, and socially isolated throughout their lives. Individuals with less severe problems may marry, but find the sexual side of marriage a continuing problem. Secondary nonsexual difficulties such as impaired self-esteem, depression, marital conflict, alcohol and tranquilizer dependence, etc., are not uncommon. Sexual phobias may also lead to secondary disorders of sexual functioning, especially inhibition of sexual desire in the afflicted person and sometimes also in his or her spouse.

The avoidance maneuvers of the sexual phobic are many and varied; one is often quite impressed by their ingenuity in avoiding feared sexual situations, as they truly become "artful dodgers." It is not at all uncommon for the true state of affairs to be unknown to the spouse! In less severe cases, afflicted individuals may rely on chemicals (alcohol, tranquilizers) to enable them to cope with the feared situation, at least on an occasional basis, then endeavoring to get "it" over with as quickly as possible. Some couples manage to work out a mutually satisfactory way of side-stepping the problem.

Whatever the reason for a particular sexual phobia developing in the first place, it can be perpetuated and maintained by what amounts to the unexpected "fringe benefits" of having the problem (technically called secondary gains), or by the individual's or partner's response to it.

For example, sexual avoidance "necessitated" by a sexual phobia may be used (not necessarily consciously and deliberately) to enhance one's feelings of control in what amounts to be a continuing marital power struggle. Giving up the symptom here would be to decrease one's control and power. Personal feelings of inadequacy or guilt because of the problem tend to make it progressively worse. Angry responses by a partner, or persistent partner pressure to perform sexually, usually worsens a sexual phobia and may lead to a spread of anxiety to other areas, or facilitate the development of some other form of sexual dysfunction.

Special Problems When You Don't Have a Partner

It is usually much easier to overcome a problem of DSD if you have a cooperative partner with whom you can thoroughly discuss all the relevant issues and work on some joint corrective exercises. This is not to deny that a great deal can be achieved by work on yourself, but it is fairly obvious that ultimately sexual confidence comes from successful involvement with a partner! Many partnerless men and women find themselves in a catch-22 situation. Until they can find a caring partner with whom they can relate sexually quite comfortably, they cannot build up their sexual confidence. Because they lack sexual confidence, they find it very difficult to get into a nonthreatening sexual situation with a partner.

I have found that generally the best solution is to form a relationship with a partner you like, and when you get to know him or her better, level with him or her about your difficulty. When you do, describe the problem positively, and not apologetically! For example, you might say, "I want you to know that I've had some minor problems in the sexual area, but I'm confident that as I get to know you better, these will go away." A new partner who does not respond sympathetically or helpfully to this type of up-front honest approach is probably not going to have much to offer you in the long haul, and you might as well find out sooner rather than later! If you do get an unsympathetic response, do not catasrophize and convince yourself that all partners will have the same response—this simply is not true! Just keep looking until you find the right one.

Most of my clients have found the direct leveling approach just described better than any other alternative with a new partner. It puts you into a no-lose situation! If he or she can't handle the situation sympathetically, he or she is not for you anyway, and you will find that out very quickly. More usually, he or she will be accepting of the situation and try to help. Having leveled, you will find that you are much less anxious when you do relate sexually.

Teach a new partner what you have learned about the key sexual attitude! You can then get to know him or her sexually at your own pace, at the same time progressively building up your sexual confidence.

Some clients I have worked with have found that they simply could not level this way with a new partner. Many of these individuals have overcome their embarrassment and anxiety about leveling by practicing saying what needs to be said into a tape recorder. They listen to what they have said, and then do it again, working to make it eventually sound just right for them and continuing until they no longer feel uncomfortable saying it.

You must remember that almost every person, man and woman alike, is a little anxious the first time they make love with a new partner. This is normal and virtually inevitable! To make sexual relating with a new partner as free from anxiety as possible, I have offered a few additional hints in appendix 3.

Treatment Issues

The Role of Specialists

The endocrinologist. This physician specializes in diseases of endocrine glands—the body structures that produce hormones. The endocrinologist is expert in diagnosing and treating hormonal disorders, but has had no special training in the overall management of sexual problems. Treatments mostly involve the use of drugs aimed at overcoming hormone problems.

The gynecologist. This specialist is a surgeon concerned with disorders of the female genitals and reproductive organs. A gynecologist has special skill in diagnosing and treating disorders of these structures. Some have a special interest in sexual functioning and are expert in the sexual problems of women.

The neurologist. This physician specializes in diseases of the brain, spinal cord, nerves, and muscles. The neurologist has had special training in the diagnosis and management of these problems, but not in the treatment of sexual disorders. When there is a treatment available for a neurological disorder, it usually involves drugs, or in some cases surgery.

The psychiatrist. This physician is concerned with the psychological aspects of medicine, and may or may not have had special training and experience in the management of sexual problems. The contribution of a psychiatrist who has such training lies in helping overcome the psychological factors contributing to or maintaining a sexual difficulty. Psychiatrists also have expertise in helping couples cope with marital or relationship problems. Before consulting with a psychiatrist about a libido problem, check with your family doctor or the psychiatrist's secretary to make sure that psychiatrist deals with sexual problems, as not all do.

The psychologist. This professional is not medically qualified and therefore has had no training in the various physical disorders and chemical agents that may contribute to libido problems.

Clinical psychologists, like psychiatrists, may have special expertise in the management of the psychological issues relevant to sexual problems. Before consulting with one, check to make sure that psychologist has had training and experience in the management of sexual problems, as not all have.

The sex therapist. Individuals who practice as sex therapists specialize in the management of sexual problems. They may or may not be medically qualified—some are by basic training clinical psychologists. Medically qualified sex therapists come from many specialties—some were family physicians, some psychiatrists, some gynecologists, and so on. Their training and experience in the sexual field is more important than their original specialty.

The urologist. This specialist is a surgeon concerned with disorders of the male genitals and the urinary system—kidneys and bladder—of both sexes. The urologist has special skill in diagnosing and treating disorders of these structures, which may be relevant to sexual desire problems.

The Role of Drugs in Managing Sexual Desire Problems

Over the centuries, a wide variety of chemical agents have been tried and recommended to enhance deficient sexual drive, although *none* have survived the rigors of scientific scrutiny. The search for an effective aphrodisiac goes on today, for as long as humans value sexual functioning there will be a demand for sex-enhancing drugs.

Male hormone. If this is administered to normal women, it often increases libido. This response is less commonly seen in normal men. On the other hand, if a man or a woman has a proven, significant deficiency of testosterone, then replacement therapy makes good sense and may improve or even cure a problem of DSD. Occasionally there is a legitimate role for the use of extra testosterone in DSD when an individual does not have any such deficiency. This is mainly as a short-term libido-booster to facilitate psychological changes, which will then hopefully perpetuate the initially stimulated sexual drive. The use of extra testosterone, over and above what the body needs, is not without its problems and risks. For example, women who take too much for too long may wind up with a persistent moustache for their troubles! Furthermore, *testosterone is by no means always effective in boosting libido,* even in the short term.

If a doctor suggests giving you testosterone as a treatment for DSD, I would urge you to decline, at least until a proper blood test has been carried out to determine whether you are in fact deficient in testosterone. If you are, then further investigations often have to be conducted to find out the cause of the problem before the diagnostic situation is confused by the administration of male hormone.

Synthetic testosterone-like drugs. The same comments apply here as with testosterone itself, but in general they are often less satisfactory than testosterone, should you genuinely need male hormone replacement.

Other hormone treatments. If your DSD is due to or associated with other hormone disorders, these will usually need some form of specific drug treatment. However, such treatments can have no beneficial effects on DSD unless you suffer from the disorder they are designed to treat.

Antidepressants. These may improve libido if DSD is associated with a depressive illness.

Minor tranquillizers. These are drugs like diazepam. They combat anxiety and are occasionally helpful in reducing it to a degree sufficient to enable predominantly anxiety-based DSD, or aversions, to be overcome. Usually they are totally unhelpful.

Anti-panic drugs. If an individual develops true panic attacks in anticipation of, or during, sexual contact as described earlier in this chapter, it may be necessary to suppress these with one of the several relatively specific anti-panic drugs available before other measures can be effective in overcoming sexual anxiety and DSD.

Marijuana and other "street" drugs. The sexual effects of marijuana and other illegal drugs are very variable. There is no doubt that for some individuals marijuana, amphetamine, and cocaine can stimulate sexual interest, although in other people the very same drugs can decrease libido. Perhaps a lot of the effect of these drugs on sexual interest relates to expectancy. They are frequently taken with the belief that they will certainly enhance sexuality! Nothing can be said in their favor as a "treatment" for DSD. Quite apart from the fact that their use is illegal and therefore can have serious social consequences, they *can all have harmful effects,* sometimes serious ones. Even marijuana is by no means as innocuous as was once believed.

Pheromones. These are substances secreted by animals which attract members of the opposite sex through their olfactory (smell) sense. Work on human pheromones is still in its infancy, but these may prove to be true aphrodisiacs and ultimately have a legitimate medical use.

The future of aphrodisiacs. There are a number of tantalizing leads into an understanding of the biochemistry of sexual drive, and it is hard to believe that sooner or later a specific, safe libido-stimulator will not be found. This may help in the management of DSD in some cases, although getting the psychological issues right will always remain important!

Drugs for problems of excessive sexual drive. A variety of commonly effective drugs are available to assist in the management of these problems in some cases. They all have potentially significant side effects, and have to be used with caution under careful medical supervision.

Hypnosis

Hypnosis is essentially a state where you are relaxed, focused mentally on what is being said, and very susceptible to appropriate suggestions. You can induce a state of hypnosis by yourself or with the assistance of a therapist. There are many different ways in which the hypnotic state can be used to assist people with DSD, and whatever approach is used by a skilled therapist will be individually tailored to the specific needs of a particular client. Hypnosis is merely one of a variety of psychological treatments that can be used in DSD, and it is most often used in conjunction with other methods rather than by itself.

What If Everything Fails?

Sometimes, despite expert help plus your own very best efforts, DSD cannot be overcome for a variety of possible reasons. Should this occur, it is not in any way the end of the world, unless you start catastrophizing and telling yourself over and over in your mind that you can in consequence never be happy or loved!

If you have an absolutely intractable aversion to sexual contact with an otherwise loved partner, all you can do is agree to completely avoid sexual contact, and concentrate on making the most of other areas of your relationship. Hopefully, your partner will then masturbate to relieve his or her sexual tensions, and you won't make yourself feel guilty or inadequate because of that! Sometimes time heals, and for no particular reason you may gradually find yourself becoming increasingly comfortable with affectionate physical contact, which might even eventually flow on to the sexual area.

If you have an insoluble problem of purely situational DSD where your libido difficulty manifests itself only toward your partner, you may be able to negotiate a reasonably satisfactory sexual compromise. For example, you make love (in the sense that I have repeatedly emphasized) when your partner is in the mood (and you are not frankly anti sexual contact) without expecting anything much to happen sexually for you. You would then persumably deal with your own sexual tension needs in private masturbation. Some people with an intractable situational DSD get around the problem by fantasizing during lovemaking that their partner is really someone else. This may be a neat, if imperfect, solution for you.

For individuals with intractable global DSD, once again it should be possible to work out a reasonably satisfactory sexual compromise along the lines I suggested in the chapter on mismatched libidos. Once you stop worrying about the fact that you are not going to be interested, responsive, or sexually fulfilled, and when you stop feeling jealous or resentful of your partner's pleasure and begin to concentrate on the emotional closeness of intimate relating, then you should be able to get something out of making love yourself, even if you never or rarely experience sexual interest or arousal. Once again, time can be a great healer, and things might gradually improve.

Whatever compromise you both have to eventually settle for, remember the following:

1. Don't put yourself down or blame yourself because of your persistent DSD. Your value and worthwhileness as a person have got *nothing whatsoever* to do with your sexual abilities, and anyway, your problem is demonstrably totally beyond your control, since you have done everything you could to overcome it. If you need help to achieve this attitude, try one of the books on attitude change listed in appendix 4.

2. You can almost always "make love," as I have defined it throughout this book, unless you have a totally intractable, severe aversion to physical contact, which is excessively rare!

3. When you finally give up trying to overcome a problem, accepting it as incurable, for the first time you can devote all your efforts to learning to live with it, and make the best possible life for you and your partner despite it! Finally giving up trying to be cured can thus be a giant step forward in happiness for you both!

4. Always strive to maximize the positive functional aspects of your relationship, so that the persistent sexual problem has the minimum possible adverse effect on your overall involvement.

5. With the rapid advance of scientific knowledge, perhaps before long there will be a breakthrough that will help you—as the old saying goes, "while there is life, there is hope"!

Maintaining Treatment Gains

Often when a couple follow the program I have outlined, there is a gratifying improvement in sexual interest during the time the partners are actively involved in working on the difficulty, thinking about it, and communicating it frequently. However, when the libido problem is felt to be cured, all of the measures described in this book abruptly cease, and the partners take the situation for granted. Sometimes when this happens, they slowly sink back into old, unhelpful ways, and effective communication about sexual needs and feelings dries up. Not surprisingly, the libido problem may start to surface once again.

Don't allow yourself to fall into this trap!

The best practical way to avoid it is to institute a weekly "state-of-the-union" session. Mutually agree that each and every week, for the rest of your life together, at a particular general time and on a particular day, you will together constructively review the state of your relationship, generally and sexually. This is often most effectively done when you are lying down having a cuddle, as this situation makes it easier and more comfortable to express dissatisfactions. The message conveyed is, "I love you and feel close to you in spite of the dissatisfactions I am expressing." Don't forget also to mention the good things you notice and feel about your relationship. Soften anything that might possibly be hurtful by introducing it something like this: "It may be completely unreasonable of me, but . . . ," or "I may be absolutely wrong, but . . . ."

If you make this weekly session, which often only takes a few minutes, a rigid, inviolable part of your weekly routine, I think you will find that little problems are recognized and dealt with promptly, before they become larger and more difficult to talk about and deal with! See this state-of-the-union session as akin to the preventative maintenance you regularly have performed on your car.

PART II

Exercise Sessions

Session 1

Approaches To Help Develop the Key Sexual Attitude

The crucial attitude, which you must work at developing, is simply this:

> Lovemaking means literally that—interacting physically and emotionally with someone you care about. Arousal, intercourse, and orgasm or ejaculation are nonessential, and simply possible lovemaking options.

The fact that most people, particularly men, find this notion a little unusual at first glance, and that more often than not for most people lovemaking does involve arousal and intercourse, do not in any way invalidate this notion.

Why Is This Attitude So Important?

Apart from being absolutely true, it is the basis of ongoing, lifelong sexual happiness, for both males and females. When you really believe it and accept it, affectionate and sexual expression become relieved of the performance concerns which cause so much misery for so many people.

A General Principle About Attitude Change

Well established, entrenched beliefs are notoriously difficult to alter. Reading about more appropriate attitudes, and logical argument are not particularly effective in changing one's established beliefs. In general, the most effective and quickest way to change an attitude is to change behavior—in other words, to actually do certain things relevant to the attitudes it is desired to change and acquire.

Developing the Key Sexual Attitude

1. Make love with your partner when he or she feels like it but you don't (as long as you don't feel *anti!*). However, do not allow yourself to become aroused, to have intercourse, or to reach orgasm. Just concentrate on the closeness and whatever physical feelings you experience, pleasurable or otherwise. If you start to feel aroused, just hold each other, or pleasure your partner, until these feelings subside. If your partner feels like having an orgasm, offer him or her a "hand job."

2. As often as you get a chance, engage in some form of gentle, direct sexual touching with your partner in situations in which there is no chance of the contact progressing to formal lovemaking. For example, when kissing goodbye as you leave for work, lovingly fondle your partner's sexual areas and ask him or her to do the same for you. Just concentrate on what you are doing and experiencing, whether you register it as pleasant or not so pleasant.

3. Each and every time you catch yourself thinking that because you are not aware of feeling interested in sex you are no good or inadequate as a partner, or similar irrational and destructive thoughts about your sexual performance, put a cross on a small note pad that you carry around at all times for this specific purpose. Do this immediately you become aware that you are having unwanted thoughts. This form of "self-monitoring" is a very effective technique for steadily decreasing the frequency of these types of thoughts. Simple, isn't it?

4. Preferably while giving your partner a nonsexual cuddle in private, explain to him or her in full detail exactly how you feel emotionally when he or she is obviously sexually interested and you aren't. Explain just how your anxiety, anger, shame, and so on affects you, what sort of thoughts you have, what you fear he or she may be thinking, what you fear he or she may do, what you fear the future may hold. As you elaborate on these emotions and irrational thoughts, keep telling your partner (and yourself) just how ridiculous it is for you to think and feel this way, and how much you tend to exaggerate the importance of actually feeling sexually interested. Do this as often as possible whenever you get the chance.

By thus repeatedly expressing your concerns and ridiculing them, you will find they will decrease. Sharing them with your partner will also help him or her to understand and assist you. Note that you are only ridiculing your ideas and beliefs, *not* yourself—you are not under any circumstances putting yourself down.

5. With your partner's help, work out and write down a comprehensive and very detailed list of all the specific advantages (for you, for your partner, for you both) of lovemaking not having to involve arousal, intercourse, or any other specific goal. These will mainly revolve around:

a. Eradicating all anxiety or concern about sexual performance, allowing you both simply to enjoy the closeness and each other with an open agenda.
b. Encouraging you to try new, not necessarily overtly sexual, forms of touching and stimulation, and to develop an entirely new approach to sensuality.

Be very specific as you list these advantages—for example:

a. We can make love whether or not we both feel sexually interested without having to worry about becoming aroused and "performing."
b. We can still make love when I feel tired without me having to worry that I might perhaps go to sleep during lovemaking.

Having worked out this list, put it away, and a few days later begin thoroughly discussing each item with your partner over a number of short sessions.

6. Teach as many other people as possible (friends, adult children, workmates) that lovemaking means just that, and there is no element of performance. It is always a success! When doing this, of course, you certainly don't have to reveal that you have a problem. It could be worthwhile, however, saying that with your partner there is no fussing if you start lovemaking when you are not really in the mood and don't become aroused, or something similar.

The general principle is that teaching someone else a new attitude is an excellent and powerful way of developing it yourself.

7. Use autosuggestion, as discussed in session 3.

8. Use the Premack principle, as discussed in session 3.

9. Whenever lovemaking is a possibility (and perhaps also during lovemaking), remind yourself of the key sexual attitude by repeatedly thinking it to yourself.

You may wonder why I have offered so many different maneuvers to help you develop the key sexual attitude. My reasons are simple—you *must* develop this attitude; achieving it is not exactly a push-over, and not every self-help technique works properly for each and every person.

If you accept my view that you must develop this attitude, *force* yourself to do as many of these exercises as possible, even if you feel uncomfortable or totally stupid! If, after a fair trial, one of these approaches somehow just doesn't seem to be helpful for you, stop doing it.

You will know when you can stop working on acquiring this key attitude—it will seem perfectly natural to you, and you will no longer be concerned or anxious about whether or not you are sexually interested or responsive.

Session 2

Thought Stopping

If *negative* or *unhelpful thoughts* tend automatically to come to your mind whenever there is a possibility of sex (for example, if you are a victim of the automatic turnoff mechanism (chapter 12)), you will tend to suppress your sexual drive. Likewise, if in a sexual situation with your partner you are thinking of unrelated issues, or about how you will perform sexually, or about what your partner will think of your performance, you will make it difficult for yourself to get aroused.

Thought stopping is a simple and effective psychological procedure for getting unwanted thoughts out of one's mind, and there are a number of different ways of doing it. The variation to be described is particularly effective in getting rid of unhelpful thoughts about sex at any time, but especially when it is a possibility or actually happening.

The Procedure

Say aloud, or if that is not possible, think to yourself:

"Stop! I'm not going to let myself think like that. It's irrational."

Then immediately imagine yourself in a standard, peaceful, relaxing scene for three seconds. While doing this, close your eyes if that is possible. If you can't, think of your peaceful scene with your eyes open for three seconds.

Some Important Points

1. Always use *exactly* the same words. Do not change them in any way.
2. Wear a thick elastic band on your wrist, and as you think "stop," give yourself a really painful flick on the wrist. If that is not possible, because it would be embarrassing, bite your tongue or cheek! This painful stimulus as you think stop will enable you to learn this technique much more rapidly. Of course, when you are an absolute expert at thought stopping, it will no longer be necessary to give yourself a painful stimulus.
3. *Always* say or think this sequence with plenty of feeling or emphasis. Unless this is done each and every time you use thought stopping, it will not work properly. *Never* allow the thought stopping sequence to become an emotional, neutral series of words.
4. Say or think this sequence at normal talking speed. Do *not* go through it too rapidly.
5. Always use *exactly* the same peaceful scene. Repeatedly practice visualizing it until it is always the same.
6. It will require perhaps several thousand practice runs until this technique is fully effective in getting rid of unwanted thoughts. Whatever you do, don't make the mistake of giving up because it hasn't worked properly after only a few hundred trials.

How To Practice Thought Stopping

1. Wear a thick elastic bank on the wrist on which you wear your watch. Whenever you look at the time, you will see the elastic band, and this will remind you to practice your thought stopping technique.
2. For a few days, only use thought stopping against trivial passing thoughts that are of no importance to you until the technique becomes automatic. When you can do it without having to think about it, do two things:
   a. Keep practicing on any trivial thoughts that come into your mind whenever you think of it. The elastic band will help to remind you to do this.
   b. Start using it against thoughts that you genuinely wish to be rid of for some reason, such as worrying or upsetting thoughts.

   When you start doing this, you will naturally find that as soon as you have finished the thought stopping sequence, the unwanted thoughts will come back. You then immediately repeat the whole sequence, performing this over and over again, if necessary, to keep the unwanted thoughts out of your mind. Even though doing this repeatedly is boring, you will have no alternative for a while. However, each time you do it over and over again, the effectiveness of the procedure will slowly and progressively increase.

Caution. *Always* put some feeling or emphasis into your thought stopping sequence no matter how many thousands of times you might have done it! *Never,* under any circumstances, allow the sequence to become mechanical or unemotional!

How To Use Thought Stopping

1. **Outside the sexual situation.** You must declare war on unhelpful thoughts about your sexual interest or performance regardless of the circumstances under which they occur! In any situation, the instant you realize that you are thinking negatively about sex, push these grossly destructive thoughts out of your mind by using thought stopping, repeating it over and over again if need be.

2. **When sex is a possibility or in a sexual situation.** Here it is absolutely essential to rid your mind of any unhelpful thoughts! These might be about negative aspects of you, or your partner, or your relationship, or about your sexual performance, or about unrelated matters such as an unresolved problem from work.

There is a simple variation of your standard thought stopping technique, which is often even more useful when you are in physical contact with your partner. It goes like this: "Stop! I'm not going to let myself think like that. It's irrational. All I have to do is concentrate on what I'm feeling now." Then concentrate all your attention on the physical sensations you experience as you are touched or as you touch your partner.

You can practice this variation of the standard thought stopping procedure on either trivial or genuinely unwanted thoughts *after* you have mastered the basic technique. When you do practice, touch yourself and concentrate on the sensations you experience. When you feel proficient, practice when you are touching or being touched by your partner in a nonsexual setting, for example, if you are holding hands while you watch TV.

Remember

1. You *must* declare war on unhelpful thoughts, especially thoughts about your sexual interest or performance, past, present, or future.

2. Until you are truly expert at this procedure, you may have to do thought stopping over and over again to keep unwanted thoughts out of

your mind. However, this is infinitely better than allowing yourself repeatedly to think destructive thoughts.

3. You *must* always use some feeling or emphasis each and every time you do thought stopping.

4. If you just keep practicing over and over again, you *must eventually* develop a powerful and effective skill for getting rid of any kind of unwanted thoughts, not just ones relevant to sex.

Note: If you have difficulty *visualizing* a peaceful scene in your mind, you might try one of the following alternatives:

1. Visualize instead a blank white wall or a STOP sign.

2. Play in your head a brief segment of your favorite music, making it always the same.

Session 3

Talking Sense to Yourself

It is impossible to emphasize strongly enough the importance of the thoughts you allow yourself to have! They substantially control and determine how you feel and what you do and say in different situations, and they can powerfully facilitate or suppress awareness of your innate sexual drive. When working to overcome a problem of deficient sexual drive, it is *crucially* important to have your thought processes going for you. Put another way, it is essential repeatedly to "talk sense to yourself" to overcome the effects of unhelpful thoughts.

I am going to describe five procedures which have rather different uses, but ultimately similar goals. They are:

1. "Coping self-statements"
2. The "observer" technique
3. "Talking sense to the unconscious"
4. The Premack principle
5. Autosuggestion

While obviously not every self-help technique is right for every person with every problem, you should find one, or even several of the above, relevant to your situation and effective in your hands. However, don't get too ambitious and try to use them all simultaneously! Some of these techniques have a particular use for individuals with situational DSD.

The "Coping Self-Statements" Technique

When soon you will be in, or when you are in, a situation that makes you "uptight" (anxious, angry, guilty, etc.), make yourself think, over and over and with "feeling," the following: "OK, so I'm (going to be) uptight, but I'm absolutely certain that I will cope with the situation."

If you reflect on your own past experience, this is true! Almost all the situations you have been uptight about in the past haven't been quite as bad as you thought they would, and you have in fact coped, in the sense that you somehow or other stumbled through and survived!
If you use this technique of acknowledging your uptightness (rather than trying to conceal or get rid of it), you will find you feel much more comfortable!

Note: For maximum benefit, you must think this repeatedly and with feeling.

The "Observer" Technique

The idea is to work at achieving this attitude:

There is the new me and the old me. The new me can observe and disengage from old unwanted automatic thoughts and feelings that will simply pass and then occur progressively less often.

Your past experiences have taught you to respond automatically with certain thoughts and feelings to various life situations without any logical evaluation. While most of these automatic responses are adaptive and helpful, some are not. One way of eliminating unwanted automatic thoughts and feelings is to observe them and simply let them pass without getting emotionally involved with them!

When you find yourself thinking and feeling in unhelpful ways, work at disengaging from them by *repeatedly* thinking to yourself: "These thoughts and feelings are just part of the old me. I will simply observe them, let them happen, let them pass. They are not important. They are just an automatic response, and they will occur progressively less frequently."

Obviously, it will take time and practice to learn to avoid getting involved with these old, unwanted automatic thoughts and feelings, but it can be done!

You can considerably enhance the efficacy of this technique by explaining to your partner what you are trying to achieve at that particular moment.

The regular practice of meditation (session 7) greatly facilitates mastery of this technique.

"Talking Sense to the Unconscious"

A moment's reflection should convince you that your mind contains a mass of memories and responses to which you are not consciously aware most of the time, or even ever. These background or "unconscious" memories and responses can and do powerfully influence you in the present! For example, if as a child your mother repeatedly bashed into you the notion that masturbation was dirty and wrong, you will as an adult tend to feel uncomfortable about masturbating, even though the memories of your mother telling you all this are rarely or never in your mind.

If you ever find yourself thinking negative, anxiety, guilt, or anger provoking thoughts about sex or about engaging in some form of normal sexual behavior, one way of combating them is to forcefully work at freeing yourself from the noxious influences of your past by, as it were, "talking sense to your unconscious" (mind).

To do this, repeatedly and with feeling think (or if appropriate, say aloud) something like this: "My mother had it all wrong about sex; she tried to wreck my sexual happiness because of her own hangups. There is nothing wrong with masturbation and I can and will enjoy it. Mother is not here now, and I'm not going to allow her to adversely influence me any longer."

If your automatic, unwanted negative thoughts and feelings result from some sexual trauma (such as rape), you might modify this format slightly as follows:

"Being raped was a terrible experience, but I'm not going to suffer even more by wrecking my sexual happiness with my partner. Sex is meant to be enjoyable, and I can and will enjoy it. I'm not going to allow the past to handicap me any longer."

Depending on the origins of your negative attitudes and feelings toward sex, you will have to modify these formats appropriately, but the general principle remains unchanged—*repeatedly* and forcefully talk sense to yourself, emphasizing that you are no longer going to allow the past to adversely affect your happiness.

The Premack Principle

This is used here as a simple, ingenious, and effective means of changing unwanted attitudes. In essence, you *force* yourself repeatedly to think whatever it is you want to believe, *with feeling,* when you are reminded to do so by some frequently occurring activity in your daily life. One of the beauties of this technique is that it is effective even if you currently believe the exact opposite of the attitude you are working at acquiring!

I will show you how to do it, using the acquisition of the key sexual attitude as an example.

Memorize this statement word for word:

> Lovemaking means literally that—interacting physically and emotionally with someone you care about. Arousal, intercourse, and orgasms are nonessential and simply possible lovemaking options!

Next, work out some frequently recurring event in your daily routine, for example, making a telephone call. *Force* yourself to say or think the above statement with the maximum possible *feeling* six times before you allow yourself to make each and every phone call. If you can't think of anything that happens frequently, link the statement to water, for example, before you allow yourself to touch water, drink water (which means any liquid at all), or pass water (urinate), first you say or think the statement six times, *with maximum feeling.*

You will find that if you do this simple maneuver regularly for a few weeks, it will greatly assist you in acquiring the desired attitude to your sexual expression. Keep using this procedure until you are quite convinced that the desired attitude is truly now your own.

Even though this sounds extremely simple and is totally contrived, you will find it very helpful indeed.

You can use this technique to help overcome the destructive effects of any persistent unwanted attitudes based on sexual myths or traumatic past experiences.

Autosuggestion

We are all suggestible—affected by what other people say to us and by the things we say to ourselves. In a relaxed state, in which our mind can more easily focus on what is being said or thought, we are much more suggestible than usual and therefore more powerfully affected by what is said or by our own thoughts.

It is easy enough to exploit your own suggestibility to your advantage by repeatedly giving yourself appropriate suggestions in a situation where these will have their maximum impact. The procedure is very simple, and I recommend its use to help you change and overcome the effects of unhelpful attitudes based on sexual myths or traumatic experiences.

How do you do it?

1. Sit comfortably in a chair, eyes closed, head slightly forward.
2. Relax yourself by using one or other of the methods described in session 6.

3. Think to yourself, slowly and with feeling, the appropriate suggestion, which you must first have memorized word for word.

For example, to help develop the key sexual attitude, you might use the following:

> "Lovemaking is just a way of showing love; there are many options and it is always a success!"

4. Repeat the suggestion six times, with feeling, then remain relaxed for about half a minute before opening your eyes. Stay seated for a further minute before you get up.

Do this simple little exercise as often as you can. With practice it will only take three or four minutes. Aim to do it at least three times daily and continue until you are completely confident that the desired attitude is yours.

You can use this technique to help overcome the effects of any destructive sexual myth or traumatic experience, but use it to tackle only one issue at a time! Wait until you feel your new attitude has been set in concrete before using autosuggestion against another sexual myth or trauma.

Here are some hints on wording suggestions:

1. Keep them *short and simple*—as though talking to a child!

2. Try to word the suggestion *positively,* and avoid negative words such as no, not, and so on.

For example, do not say something like this: "I do not have to be sexually interested to make love, even without it, lovemaking can still be successful." Note that the overall tone of this suggestion is *negative.* You would have turned it into a *positive* suggestion if you changed it to this: "Sexual interest is totally unnecessary during lovemaking and lovemaking is always a success."

With a little practice, ANY suggestion can be worded positively!

3. Always write down the suggestion you propose to use, and then check to make sure the above two rules have been obeyed. When you have it right (short, simple, and positive), memorize it word for word before using it in this exercise.

4. Use only one suggestion each time. Don't get ambitious and attempt to give yourself several suggestions when you use this technique.

Session 4

Additional Exercises To Overcome the Effects of Destructive Sexual Myths

Over and above the specific procedures listed in chapter 6, you can adapt some of the "doing" exercises described in session 1 to help you overcome the effects of some personally particularly destructive myth.

You can, for example, as an exercise *deliberately* engage in some form of sexual behavior with the proviso that whatever you have previously believed should occur must under no circumstances be allowed to occur. For example, if as a man you are working to overcome the destructive effects of the myth that males must always be active during sex, make a deal with your partner that as an exercise sexual contact will occur where she will be responsible for absolutely everything. You will remain totally passive, quite literally doing nothing until and unless you are given a firm instruction to do something to or for her.

Self-monitoring (session 1, exercise 3) is very useful in tackling almost any myth (or automatic illogical way of thinking) that you wish to overcome. However, *only* use it against *one* myth at a time. If you are using it against a couple of sexual myths simultaneously, you will make the technique less effective.

Discussing in detail with your partner your irrational feelings or emotions associated with and based on a myth can be very helpful, as described in session 1, exercise 4. Likewise, teaching and persuading others that the myth is truly absurd (session 1, exercise 6) is a powerful procedure for helping yourself.

The Premack principle and autosuggestion are widely applicable and helpful, but as with self-monitoring, only use them against one particular myth at a time! Don't forget to rewrite the myth in logical terms when you use these two procedures. The observer technique also has a wide applicability. These three procedures are described in session 3.

Session 5

Self-Monitoring

This is a technique with two important uses:

1. To gather vital information that you can use to help yourself.
2. As a simple treatment to change unwanted automatic patterns of thinking.

Self-Monitoring for Important Data

1. Each day, record in a small notebook kept for this purpose your estimate of your self-perceived sexual drive or interest. Do this once a day in the evening, but before you are too tired. Give yourself a daily score between one and ten. One means absolutely no awareness at any stage of even the slightest degree of sexual interest. Ten means a very clear-cut awareness of a definite sexual interest, even if very short-lived. With practice, you will be able to judge in-between scores. After each day's score, write down anything you can think of that happened that day which might have influenced or contributed to your day's score. This could refer to some external happening, such as a worrysome event or a movie, or to reactions, thoughts, or feelings in you. It certainly includes the practice of the various exercises in this book! Should you forget to fill in your record on a particular day, do *not* try to fill it in from memory the next day—just leave a blank.

It is advisable to continue this daily recording for the entire period of time you spend working on your self-help program. Not only will it give you important and practical useful insights into the factors influencing your sexual interest, but it will give you a concrete idea of your progress. You will usually also come to realize that you are more often thinking about and tuned in to your sexual nature than you had previously thought.

2. Whenever sexual contact with a partner is either a possibility or an actuality, pay close attention to the thoughts you have in your mind. For a moment or two, stand outside yourself, as it were, and note what thoughts you are having. As soon as practicable after the possibility or event has passed, write down in a different section of your notebook the general kinds of thoughts you were having. Note both *positive* and *negative* thoughts. Doing this will make you acutely aware of just how much the thoughts you allow yourself to have influence the way you feel. It will also remind you of your need to "talk sense to yourself" (session 3).

Self-Monitoring as Treatment

The general principle is this: If you record (in writing) the occurrence of any specific unwanted thought or piece of behavior immediately after it occurs, it will occur progressively less often. Note the crucial importance of the word "immediately."

Decide from "self-monitoring for important data," step 2 above, what general kinds of thoughts (relevant to sex) recurrently cause problems for you. Summarize these in the third section of your self-monitoring notebook. Then record an X in this part of the notebook immediately when you catch yourself thinking thoughts like these. Do this every single time you become aware of these thoughts, even if it means you have to repeatedly take your notebook out to make yet another X! It is no good making a mental note. For this technique to be fully effective, it must be a written X! Note that by studying the day-by-day accumulation of Xs, you will also be getting a clear idea of your progress in the struggle against these destructive thoughts.

Remember, even though these three applications of self-monitoring are very simple, they are extremely important! As previously mentioned, it is impossible to over-emphasize the importance of the kinds of thoughts we allow ourselves to have. Thoughts have a *profound* effect on our awareness of our innate sexual drive and on our comfort in expressing this drive.

Session 6

Self-Relaxation

Why should you master relaxation skills if you have deficient sexual drive?

1. You can't afford to be anxious or tense in a sexual situation if you are to have a chance of responding adequately.
2. You can't be simultaneously anxious and relaxed! They are incompatible states and cannot co-occur, just as you can't have ice floating around in boiling water! You can therefore use relaxation to get rid of anxiety and tension.
3. If you feel that life in general is stressful, you can use regular formal relaxation as a way of reducing the harmful effects of this stress on your libido.
4. Basic skills in formal relaxation will be needed as a prelude to "desensitization" (session 8) should this be necessary in your case, as determined in chapter 17.

I am going to describe two unrelated methods of self-relaxation, as different individuals often find one or the other more effective or more suitable for their own particular circumstances.

Method 1: Progressive Muscular Relaxation

Practice this lying down in a comfortable position, eyes closed, clothing completely loose (for example, shoes off, tie off, belt undone). Let your breathing come and go as it chooses—*do not deliberately breathe deeply or in any particular way.*

Focus mentally on your feet. Visualize them in your mind's eye, or simply think of them. Then deliberately tense the muscles of your feet, making them as tight as possible without causing any discomfort. Try to to this without actually moving your feet. When these muscles are as tight as you can comfortably make them, just let go and allow them to completely relax. As you let them relax, repeatedly think to yourself, silently in your mind, each time you breathe out, "relax."

When the feet muscles feel completely relaxed, stop thinking relax as you breathe out, and focus mentally on your calf muscles. Tense them as much as you can comfortably without actually moving your legs. When they are as tense as you can comfortably make them, just let go of the tension, again thinking to yourself, silently in your mind, each time you breathe out, relax.

When the calf muscles feel fully relaxed, repeat the process with your thigh muscles, then your jaw muscles, then your forehead muscles, then your arm muscles, then your forearm and hand muscles. When your hand muscles have been allowed to relax, pretend that you are in a standard imaginary peaceful scene (for example, lying on a beach) and keep thinking relax as you breathe out. Continue imagining yourself in this scene, thinking relax as you breathe out, for about a minute.

You should find that initially this exercise takes about 10 to 15 minutes. Once you've got the hang of doing it so you don't have to think much about what you do next or how you do it, you will find that at the end of the exercise you will feel relaxed, increasingly so with repeated practice.

Always imagine exactly the same peaceful scene at the end. This is very important. With repeated practice of the exercise, that standard scene will become a trigger signal to relax. Then when you imagine it and repeatedly think relax as you breathe out without any preliminary muscle tensing and relaxing, you will very quickly become relaxed.

With regular practice, you can eventually run through the whole exercise in about seven minutes. If possible, practice twice daily until you have thoroughly mastered it and additionally can quickly relax yourself simply by thinking relax as you breathe out, imagining your peaceful scene. You can then scale down the practice and maintain your relaxation skills by doing the actual exercise once or twice per week, most conveniently in bed just before you go to sleep at night.

To get rid of anxiety or tension in anticipation of or during lovemaking or in any other situation, simply close your eyes, imagine yourself in your standard peaceful scene, and think relax each time you breathe out. If you can't close your eyes, think of yourself in your standard peaceful scene with your eyes open, and keep thinking relax each time you breathe out.

Method 2: A Breathing Technique

Practice seated comfortably in a chair with your head hanging forward, or when you are lying down. Close your eyes and focus mentally on your lower chest and upper stomach.

Take a *very* shallow breath in, *thinking* silently in your mind, "one." Then take an equally shallow breath out, also thinking one. Make your next breath in also shallow, but just a little deeper, thinking "one and two." Then breathe out, also thinking one and two. The next breath in will be just a little deeper, and you will think "one and two and three," the same when you breathe out. The next breath in and out will be a little deeper, as you think one to four, the next even deeper, as you think one to five, and so on, until you finally reach the deepest breath you can take. When this has occurred, on your next breath in, go right back to the beginning of this sequence. In other words, take a *very* shallow breath in and out, thinking one, and repeat the sequence, progressively increasing the depth of breathing up to your maximum. Continue thus for about three to five minutes, but don't formally time yourself by using a watch—just guess when the practice time is up.

You will find that it takes a little while to get the hang of breathing this way, but it is not really difficult. When you can breathe this way without having to think too much about it, you will find yourself beginning to relax.

You will discover that with repeated practice you can breathe this way and quickly relax yourself without having to think the numbers. You should certainly practice until you can in fact easily do this, even with your eyes open.

Practice for up to five minutes at a time as often as you can until you can quickly relax yourself, within one to two minutes, using this procedure. When you can do this, maintain your skill by practicing for a few minutes just before you go to sleep at night, several times each week.

If you feel anxious or tense in anticipation of or during lovemaking, or in any other situation, use this breathing technique to quickly relax away the unwanted feelings, repeating it should they recur. With diligent practice, this should eventually be quite easy to achieve.

Note: You can, of course, use relaxation skills to combat "uptight" feelings other than anxiety, such as anger.

Session 7

Meditation

Many different types of meditation exist, but the ingredient common to all is the limiting of awareness to a simple unchanging activity and a withdrawal of attention from other thoughts. Whatever technique is used, the benefits are the same. Because various philosophical or religious concepts are sometimes associated with at least certain types of meditation and can "muddy the water," a much better term is simply *"attention training."* This describes the essential feature of meditation.

What are the beneficial effects of attention training?

1. It relaxes your body.
2. It reduces anxiety.
3. It combats the adverse effects of stress.
4. It teaches you how to get control over your thoughts. By learning to control your attention, you can then choose what thoughts you will attend to, rather than be often at the mercy of unhelpful thoughts.

Learning to Meditate

You will need to practice twice daily, every day, for 20 minutes if possible. The room where you practice should be reasonably quiet, and there must be guaranteed freedom from interruption!

The best times to practice are soon after you get up, in the morning, and in the early evening. If possible, meditate on an empty stomach. Try to avoid getting involved in other activities immediately after meditation—give yourself a little time out afterwards.

Practice sitting down, not lying. Use whatever posture you find comfortable, although your head should be slightly forward and your legs should be uncrossed. Loosen any tight clothing and take off your glasses. Feel free during meditation to adjust your position.

1. Close your eyes lightly.

2. Let your breathing come any way it wants. Do not breathe deeply or artificially.

3. Mentally scan your body from your head to your toes, making any necessary adjustments to relieve obvious muscle tension.

4. As you find yourself breathing in, *think* to yourself, silently in your mind, "one." Then, as you find yourself breathing out, *think* to yourself, silently in your mind, "go." Spread the word go out for as long a time as possible. Repeat these same thoughts each and every time you breathe in and out. Note that the words are not to be subvocalized by silently moving your lips and tongue. They are simply to be thoughts in your mind.

5. Handling other thoughts is the difficult part of learning to meditate. You are trying to learn to ignore and be unaffected by other thoughts, and simply to attend to one and go. Do *not* under any circumstances actively try to force other thoughts out of your mind! If you leave them alone and keep your attention on your meditation activity, they will soon go. You will find that initially you will repeatedly wander away from your meditative activity—this is normal and expected! When you do, as soon as you are aware of it simply bring yourself back to your meditation. Do not upset yourself or worry over these inevitable lapses of concentration. Always remember that the whole process is meant to be absolutely effortless! You are not *trying to do* anything. The aim is not to drive out all other thoughts, but to develop the ability to be unattentive to, and unaffected by, whatever thoughts and images may find their way into your mind.

6. After repeating the one/go sequence for 20 minutes (guess this, don't time it), stop this and sit with your eyes closed for about a minute, then with your eyes open for about another minute. Avoid then jumping up and immediately getting involved in some new activity! Have at least a few minutes "time out."

Possible Problems

1. After a practice session, you may feel a sense of failure because you don't feel calm or relaxed, or because you found it hard to keep your

attention on your meditative activity and ignore other thoughts.

Remember:

a. While relaxation is a frequent by-product of meditation, it is not essential and certainly not a goal to strive for! The correct mental attitude to outcome is this: "Whatever happens, happens and whatever doesn't happen, simply doesn't happen, and it doesn't matter at all."

b. Everyone initially finds it hard to keep their attention exclusively on one and go. You will gradually learn to do so if you gently, without upsetting yourself, repeatedly bring yourself back to it whenever you realize your attention has strayed.

2. You may occasionally experience what amount to tension-release phenomena. Physical tension-release may lead to involuntary movements of one kind or another, including occasional and quite violent jerks. Emotional tension-release may cause you a sudden feeling of anxiety, or consist of disturbing thoughts or mental pictures. While these experiences may be unpleasant, they are completely harmless! Always adhere to the attitude "whatever happens, happens," and just passively let it happen.

Possible Modifications

If after a fair trial you find that you have the ability to think one/go without interfering with your attention to the various thoughts passing through your mind, modify your meditation in one or both of the following ways.

1. When you breathe in, instead of always thinking one, count progressively backwards from 100 by 1 (or 2 or 3). In other words, with your first breath in, think 100. With your second breath in, think 99, and so on. Keep repeating this sequence over and over.

2. Clench your fists lightly as you breathe in and think one and very slowly release the tension as you breathe out and think go.

How Long Does It Take To Master Meditation?

Usually a few months. You may find yourself experiencing *some* of the benefits before then, perhaps even within two to three weeks. Increasing mastery will be seen in your decreasing involvement with passing thoughts.

Session 8

Desensitization

This is a simple and effective technique for overcoming inappropriate anxiety, guilt, anger, and so on—those feelings that are interfering with your ability to be in touch with your innate sexual drive, or to express it in lovemaking with a partner or in masturbation when you don't have a partner.

The principle of desensitization is very simple: If, while deeply relaxed, you repeatedly *imagine* some situation that in real life has made or makes you inappropriately anxious (or guilty, ashamed, and so on), you will gradually and progressively cease being inappropriately anxious (or guilty, etc.) in the current real-life situation.

How To Perform Desensitization

First, work out and write down a series of brief scenes covering typical examples of past actual sexual situations in which you have been anxious, guilty, angry, etc. Write these in the present tense, as though they were actually happening now.

For example:

1. "I am preparing the evening meal and thinking that tonight John will probably want me to have sex with him."
2. "Mary is snuggling up to me in bed, obviously wanting to make love. I'm just not in the mood."

Keep each scene as short as in my examples, and do *not* include in the scene how you felt. For example, do *not* say " . . . and I feel very nervous, guilty, and humiliated."

Make sure you include in your list of scenes examples of *all* the various relevant situations in which you have ever had negative emotions (anxiety, guilt, shame, anger, etc.) about the possibility or actuality of sex, including just thinking about it, avoiding it, and doing it. If you are using the technique to lay to rest past relevant traumas, review the instructions under the heading "desensitization" in chapter 17. The general rule is to be comprehensive—it is better to have too many scenes rather than too few.

Next, work out and write down a similar series of scenes, this time covering possible future situations which you have not actually experienced but could perhaps encounter some time in the future, and which would make you anxious, guilty, and so on were they to happen now. This is especially important if currently you do not have a regular partner.

For example:

"I am with a new partner having a cuddle. He obviously wants to make love."

"I'm making love with a new partner for the first time. She is very aroused and wanting intercourse, but I'm not hard enough. She is becoming frustrated with me."

Next, having worked out your list of scenes, write them down on small cards (say about the size of an appointment card), one scene per card. You are now ready to begin practicing desensitization. Proceed as follows:

1. Lie down in private in a quiet place where you will not be disturbed. Have your pile of cards nearby so they can be easily turned up, one at a time, and read. The pile of cards can be in any order. They do not, for example, have to be in sequence from the first time the problem occurred through to the present and then the future.

2. Relax yourself with your eyes closed, using one of the techniques suggested earlier. When you feel reasonably relaxed, gently, without losing your relaxation, turn up the first card and read it. Then put it down separate from the main pile, close your eyes again, and try to imagine whatever situation was described on that card. Do your best to pretend that whatever was described is actually happening now. Do *not* just vaguely remember it or see it in your mind as though you were watching it happen on a movie screen. As soon as you are aware that in any way you are beginning to lose your relaxation, stop imagining and re-relax yourself. Do not wait until imagining the situation makes you actually anxious, uneasy, tense, or uncomfortable. Stop imagining at the very first sign that you are starting to lose your relaxation.

3. When you again feel reasonably relaxed, re-imagine the same scene as though it were actually happening. Stop imagining it, and again relax

yourself at the first sign of loss of relaxation. Repeat this process with the same scene until imagining it vividly, as though it were actually happening, simply does not concern you in any way at all! When you can do this with the scene on the first card, move to the second card, doing the same thing. Should any scene not cause you to lose your feeling of relaxation the very first time you imagine it vividly, proceed directly to the next card.

4. If possible, perform this procedure for about 20 minutes each practice session, but certainly for no longer. If, however, you can only manage perhaps 10 to 15 minutes, this is still worthwhile. A lesser period than 10 minutes is not practicable.

It is quite possible that in a single practice session you may not become totally comfortable repeatedly imagining one particular scene. It may still cause you to lose your relaxation by the end of the session. Should this occur, simply resume the next practice period using the same scene.

5. Repeat this exercise, if possible on a daily or even twice daily basis, until you have worked through the entire pack of cards, so that when you imagine them, none of the scenes in any way causes you to begin to lose your relaxation. When you have finished the first run through all the cards, start again from the beginning just to be absolutely sure that none of the scenes worries you in any way.

When you have completely and correctly finished this exercise, you will find that your feelings of anxiety, guilt, and so on about sexual expression have disappeared, or are very much less!

Note: You can also use desensitization to help overcome irrational feelings of anxiety, anger, guilt, shame, disgust, or jealousy, of any origin, which may be contributing to your sexual problem.

Real-life Desensitization

If after finishing imaginal desensitization as described above you still feel somewhat uneasy about some form of actual sexual behavior, then take the desensitization technique one step further—into the real-life situation.

Write down all the individual pieces of logically desired sexual behavior that you still feel uncomfortable about. Then arrange them in order from least to most anxiety, etc., provoking. Then as an exercise, involving your partner when relevant, deliberately engage in the first (least upsetting) action or activity on your list. If you *start* to feel anxious or in any other way "uptight," immediately and formally relax yourself, and then try again. Keep going until that activity no longer makes you in any way anxious or uptight. When you have done this, move on to the next item on your list. Sessions should last 10 to 20 minutes, and it may take several or even many sessions devoted to just one activity until you no longer experience any anxiety, etc.

Session 9

Elaborated Writing

This is a self-help technique for laying the past to rest, used here when some important traumatic experience or experience in the past contributes to your problem of deficient sexual desire.

The notion is that while you can never forget the past, you can certainly prevent it continuing to have an adverse effect upon you in the present. In other words, you can neutralize it, or "lay it to rest."

When something traumatic happens to you, it generates a mixture of very powerful feelings. These feelings remain, as it were, locked up inside you until you get them out. While retained, they cause problems for you. Laying the past to rest involves getting these feelings out.

The Technique

Write out in great detail what happened when the traumatic event occurred, including the things or events that immediately preceded the trauma, and those relevant upsetting events that followed it. Write the sequence in the present tense, as though it is happening now. As you write, describe in as much detail as possible your feelings, both emotions (such as anxiety, anger, etc.) and physical feelings (such as a knot in the stomach, palpitations, etc.). Minute details of events are far less important than these feelings.

Obviously, very often you won't be able to remember the event and your reaction to it in such great detail. When you can't recall, simply guess how you probably felt or what probably happened.

As you write, allow yourself to experience whatever emotions emerge. This is absolutely crucial! You might, for example, pause from your writing, close your eyes, visualize whatever is upsetting you, and stay with whatever feelings emerge! Let yourself cry, be anxious, experience anger, etc. Don't hold back!

Keep going on your narrative as long as you can. It might vary from 20 minutes to several hours. When you have had enough, put it away for another session. In the next session, resume where you left off.

If despite your best efforts doing this exercise doesn't stir up actual emotions in you, simply *quit.* If you quit, do *not* feel you have in any way failed. Remember, no technique is always right for every person with every problem.

This exercise is meant to upset you! You have to be distressed to get the locked-up feelings out! Even though the correct practice of the procedure may be upsetting, this is only a temporary state of affairs, and before very long when all the bottled up emotions have been discharged, you will feel much better!

When you have completely finished your first account of the traumatic event, put it aside for a few days. Then reread it and underline any portions of the narrative that in any way still upset you. Then take each bit of the original narrative that still upsets you and expand it into much greater detail, following exactly the same guidelines as applied for your first effort. When you have finished this first series of elaborations, put them away for a few days before rereading them. Once again, underline any portions that still upset you, and then elaborate on or blow up each of these portions exactly as before. Continue repeating the whole process until reading your final elaboration no longer distresses you in any way!

The whole procedure may consume in total only a few hours, or it may require dozens of hours to complete. It takes as long as it takes, the goal being to get all the feelings out! When no aspect of the traumatic event in any way troubles you as you review it, it has, for practical purposes, been laid to rest and should no longer have a significant, ongoing adverse effect upon you.

Sometimes you will not know the details of the traumatic event, for example, if you once discovered your partner was having an affair. While you now know about it, you probably don't know the blow-by-blow details of what actually happened, for example, during lovemaking. In such a case, decide what aspect of the situation upsets you most, and write down an imaginary description of what you think or fear may have happened. For example, in the case of an affair, you might describe in detail your fantasy of what happened during lovemaking. Even though it is only a fantasy, you will probably find it just as upsetting as if you did know the gory details, and anyway, the only object of the exercise is to let your feelings out!

The following extract from the first elaborated writing exercise of a woman whose sexual aversion was based on a traumatic rape hopefully illustrates the technique.

> *I'm being held down by my throat. I'm aware of his huge hand around my neck; it feels as though I'm choking, I can't breathe properly. I'm absolutely terrified; my heart is pounding in my chest. I can smell his filthy breath as he tries to kiss me; I feel total revulsion as well as panic . . .*

Note that this sequence included the events that led to her being in this situation. It also included the upsetting events following it, which included giving evidence in court months later.

Caution: For some people, logic would appear to dictate that this type of upsetting, active remembering will make matters worse. I can assure you on the basis of a great deal of professional experience with this technique that this is not so! When successful, however, you may feel temporarily worse for the period you are doing the exercise. This is normal, inevitable, and indeed how the technique works (i.e., by getting the feelings out).

Session 10

Pelvic Muscle Exercise

This exercise will develop and strengthen those muscles in and around your pelvis, which are extremely important for your optimal sexual functioning. By regularly and repeatedly focusing your attention on your genital area and its functioning, it will also help you become more aware of your innate sexual nature. You may find as a bonus that your erectile and orgasmic performance is increased!

Step 1. When you urinate, practice repeatedly stopping and starting the stream of urine. When you can easily do this, learn to do it *without in any way using your stomach muscles!* Put one hand firmly over your lower abdomen to make sure these muscles are not moving to assist in stopping the flow of urine.

Step 2. When the first step has been mastered, practice exactly the same movement when you are not urinating. Practice 10 times in a row, three times daily. Gradually, over a few weeks, steadily increase until you can do it approximately 100 times in a row, three times daily. It is a good idea to discipline yourself to do this exercise each time you have a meal. This will remind you to do it, and as it is an exercise you should do for the rest of your life, it will become an automatic routine at meal times. Some people prefer to make a habit of doing it 10 to 20 times on the hour, every hour.

Until you have overcome your problem of DSD, whenever you practice this exercise focus mentally on the physical sensations you are experiencing in your genitals. This is crucially important.

Session 11

Sensuality Training Exercises

A crucial skill in overcoming any sexual problem, be it deficient sexual interest or something else, is the ability to tune in to the sensory impressions you are receiving. The exercises that follow will help you develop this skill.

Step 1. Learning to focus on skin sensations. Close your eyes and touch yourself on some exposed part of your body. See if you can focus mentally on the temperature—is it warm or cold? Then focus on the pressure feeling—is it light or firm? Then focus on the texture—is it smooth or rough? Finally, focus on the presence or absence of moisture—is it absolutely dry or is there some moisture present?

Practice this for only 10 to 20 seconds at a time, whenever you think of it, until it is very easy for you to quickly focus mentally on these four basic sensations, one after the other, whenever you touch yourself on any part of your body.

When you have become proficient at doing this, take it a step further and learn to "lose yourself" in the sensations you are feeling as you touch yourself with your eyes closed. This means learning to concentrate on these feelings to such an extent that you are totally unaware of anything else—in other words, you have no thoughts about any other thing, no awareness of anything around you. You will find that mastering this skill takes quite a lot of practice, so don't be discouraged when it turns out to be harder than you think! Practice for several minutes at a time as often as possible.

When you have *thoroughly* mastered these basic skills, then, and only then, progress to step 2.

Step 2. Focusing on and losing yourself in other sensations. Gather together some articles with a different feel, such as fur, velvet, feathers, plastic, butter, an orange, and so on. With your eyes closed, practice lightly touching these while you focus mentally on the physical sensations produced. Once again, aim to "lose yourself" in the feelings so that you have all your mental processes focused on the sensations you are experiencing to the complete exclusion of everything else. See if you can hold this exclusive focus for a few minutes at a time. Repeat this exercise using different materials, doing it as often as possible until it is easy.

Step 3. Verbalizing physical sensations. Repeat step 2, using a variety of different objects, but now say aloud to yourself exactly what you are feeling! You will discover that it is not easy to put words to physical sensations, and that considerable frequent practice is required. Nonetheless, the effort is more than worthwhile, as the skills involved are extremely important for maximizing your potential for arousal during sexual contact.

Step 4. Losing yourself in visual, olfactory (**smell**), **gustatory** (**taste**), **and auditory** (**hearing**) **sensations.** Select some printed scene or picture, or some pleasant-looking object. Then close your eyes and visualize it in your mind's eye. Learn to lose yourself in this mental picture; focus all your thought processes on it so that you are aware of nothing else. See if you can learn to hold this internal visual concentration for a few minutes at a time.

When you can easily do this, master the same skill using the other kinds of sensations. With your eyes closed, focus on a pleasant smell and try to hold on to this alone so that you are aware of nothing else. Do the same with an agreeable taste in your mouth, and finally with some appealing music or other sound.

A common response to my suggesting these exercises is that they are stupid (and Williams is mad!). While, as always, you are entitled to your own view, my experience in helping sexually dysfunctional people has convinced me of two things:

1. Most people do not know how to focus on and lose themselves in pleasant sensations.

2. The ability to focus on and lose oneself in pleasant sensations is one of the most important skills needed to overcome sexual problems and to maximize one's sexual potential.

I don't ask you to believe me, but I do ask that you give me the benefit of the doubt and diligently practice what I have asked! If you do this conscientiously and thoroughly, you will find that a whole new dimension of physical awareness is opened up to you, and that this will enhance both your sexual interest and enjoyment.

Do yourself a favor and give all these exercises a damn good try!

Session 12

Fantasy Exercises

The nature and function of sexual fantasies were discussed in chapter 3. Let me here summarize the key issues.

1. A sexual fantasy is just a series of thoughts about a sexual subject not actually happening right now. This may be completely hypothetical or imaginary, an actual past experience, about something engaging our attention at this moment, or about some realistic possibility for the future.
2. A fantasy may additionally involve mental pictures, but does not have to do so.
3. A fantasy can be very brief, even transitory.
4. We all have sexual fantasies.
5. Sexual fantasies can be pleasurable or negative.
6. We exercise *complete control* over our sexual fantasies—we write the script and we can start them or stop them when we choose.
7. Sexual thoughts (fantasies) profoundly influence psychological motivation for sex.

Why Is This Subject So Important for You?

You will find that if you learn how to use sexual fantasies to your advantage between, before, and during lovemaking, it will very powerfully assist you with your problem of deficient sexual desire. However, before you can benefit fully from the constructive use of sexual fantasy, you need to know a few more facts and to do some practice.

Some Relevant Facts

1. Just as it is normal for you to have thoughts about food, eating, and drinking from time to time during the day, so too is it normal to have thoughts about sex periodically during the day. Such thoughts are not meant to be locked up, rarely or never to see the light of day! Never having pleasant thoughts about sex from time to time is a most abnormal state. It is something largely of your own doing as you have the potential to control what you think about and a clear choice as to whether you choose to exercise that potential.

2. The kinds of sexual thoughts (fantasies) that appeal to or arouse different individuals, both men and women, are extremely variable, in the same way that we all have different favorite foods. Some people are aroused by imagining sexual activities that other equally normal people are put off about, or even find revolting! The same could be said for food. The crucial thing to understand is that whatever sexual thoughts or imaginings appeal to you, that is normal and fine. Thoughts are only thoughts and can't be abnormal! Only actual *"doing"* behavior can be abnormal, and there is a world of difference between thinking about or imagining something and actually doing it.

3. Imagining something does not put you at dire risk of doing it! Should you be concerned that if you allow your erotic imagination free reign you might be unfaithful, or become promiscuous, or lose control of yourself sexually, stop worrying. You will continue to exercise your normal control over your behavior.

4. Many women, perhaps even a majority, *need* to use a deliberate fantasy of some kind during lovemaking with their partner, at least occasionally, if they are to have any chance of becoming aroused enough to reach orgasm. This is absolutely normal! Women seem to actually need deliberate sexual fantasy during lovemaking much more than men, although as men get older, they too increasingly *need* deliberate fantasy to override some of the effects of ageing.

5. Contrary to a popular misconception, it is simply not true that an arousing sexual fantasy has to involve you with a different partner or performing unusual or amazing sexual acts. For example, many find their most arousing fantasies involve a mental replay of a past, very enjoyable lovemaking session with their present partner. Others find most arousing the thought of conventional sexual activity with their present partner, but under different, perhaps more romantic, circumstances, such as being alone on an island paradise.

6. There is absolutely no reason why you must share your sexual thoughts (fantasies) with your partner, just as there is absolutely no rational reason why you must share any other kinds of thoughts with him or her! Equally, of course, there is no law stating that you must not share your sexual thoughts (fantasies) with your partner. It is simply your choice.

7. You just can't expect to get the full benefit from the deliberate use of sexual fantasy until you have practiced and developed the skill. After all, first you have to learn to be quite comfortable within yourself about having sexual thoughts or fantasies. Then you have to learn how to use fantasies constructively to promote sexual interest and arousal. Finally you have to master the complex skill of fantasizing while you are actually making love (or masturbating) and at the same time focusing on your own physical sensations! It is something like learning to play three musical instruments all at the same time.

Learning To Use Sexual Fantasy to Your Advantage

1. In private, think of the most exciting imaginary sexual situations you can possibly dream up. Let your imagination have a field day, bearing in mind that in fantasy absolutely anything goes. Make a note of the kinds of sexual activities and situations you find most arousing. If you want some ideas, read one of the books on sexual fantasy listed in appendix 4. Remember my words to the effect that an arousing fantasy does *not* have to involve you with a different partner or performing unusual or amazing sexual acts! There is absolutely nothing wrong with this of course, but it is not in any way compulsory.

2. Next, in private, while seated or lying, select one of your exciting imaginary sexual situations, and with your eyes closed develop an *ongoing* fantasy. This will be a story involving you, with a beginning, a middle, and an end. Make sure it lasts at the very least for a few minutes. As you fantasize, try to pretend that it is actually happening to you now. If you have difficulty fantasizing in this way, it may help to start by looking at some erotic pictures or by reading some appropriately arousing material. Once you are into the swing of it, you can close your eyes to develop your own mental pictures. With practice, you will find you no longer need any aid to begin vivid fantasizing.

Repeat this exercise as often as possible, using in sequence several of the different fantasy situations and activities that most appeal to you. Remember, do a little often, rather than spend a long time at this task infrequently! Should you have difficulty visualizing an appealing fantasy in your mind, you might try imagining the physical sensations that accompany the thoughts that make up the fantasy.

With practice, you will find that you can actually tune in to a private screening of one of your favorite fantasies when you are occupied in some tedious, nondemanding activity, such as commuting, ironing, and so on. Make a conscious, deliberate effort to turn to a pleasing sexual fantasy whenever you get an opportunity, and certainly each and every day.

3. When it is easy to run through a small repertoire of pleasing or arousing fantasies in your mind, begin using them during lovemaking or masturbation. Remember, it takes some considerable practice to be able to concentrate on a fantasy while you are making love (or masturbating) and also to focus on your physical feelings! It often helps to pretend that the sensations you are actually experiencing are really being produced by whatever is happening in the fantasy, this being especially important if you find it hard to actually visualize it in your mind.

You will probably find it easiest and most effective to use those fantasies that you have been rehearsing in private. Should you feel a little uncomfortable, perhaps even guilty, about using fantasies during lovemaking with your partner, simply press on! You will find that the inappropriate and completely irrational anxiety or guilt feelings will soon disappear with continued practice.

You will find, incidentally, that the deliberate use of rehearsed sexual fantasy is combined with some of the exercises specifically directed at overcoming your problem.

4. Discuss the whole issue of sexual fantasy with your partner. A nonembarrassing way to start would be to read the end of chapter 3 and this appendix, together! Ascertain his or her views, misconceptions, and any anxieties. Then consider reading together and discussing one of the books on sexual fantasy listed in appendix 4. When you have done this, perhaps you will feel like swapping some of your favorite fantasies with your partner!

Always remember that what is good and right for one person, may not be for another. Should your partner feel uncomfortable or negative about the whole issue of sexual fantasy, naturally you must respect his or her views. However, under no circumstances then make the mistake of giving up personally on the deliberate use of fantasy; there is *absolutely* no reason why you should, even if it doesn't seem right for your partner.

Because you have a problem of deficient sexual interest, you should expect to feel uncomfortable with or, minimally, disinterested in sexual imaginings. In spite of this, make yourself do what I have suggested. Remember, the way to change faulty attitudes is to change behavior. Do *not* personally quit on practicing fantasies until you are at least quite comfortable with deliberate sexual imaginings, even if they don't do much for you!

You owe youself at least this!

Using Fantasy in Overcoming Situational DSD

As discussed in chapter 11, some individuals with DSD only experience the problem in relation to the very partner they love. Many such people have intuitively learned to use fantasy as a way of getting around the difficulty in practice, for example, during lovemaking they pretend their partner is really someone else. While there is nothing intrinsically wrong with this, some people feel dissatisfied with this state of affairs. If you are, try the following.

1. During lovemaking (or masturbation), use your usual fantasy (of someone else) until you are very nearly at orgasm. Then deliberately imagine you are with your real partner while you climax! With repeated practice of this maneuver over a long period of time, you will find that you can stop the unwanted fantasy further and further away from your orgasm, until eventually you may not need it at all! This is a technique called "orgasmic reconditioning."

2. Many times each and every day *make* yourself think of you making love with your partner and imagine enjoying it! Make these repeated fantasies very brief to begin with, allowing them to expand in time as you find it easier. Remind yourself to do this by modification to the Premack principle described in session 3.

Note: While effective, both these procedures require a lot of practice over a long period of time. Don't quit merely because they don't seem to have helped in just a few weeks.

Fantasy as an Antidote to Sexual Boredom or Monotony

The best way to prevent boredom is change, and one of the easiest changes to effect is simply to use fantasy! This, of course, is not to say that this should be the *only* variation in your lovemaking.

Session 13

Guided Imagery

This is a technique for rehearsing in imagination a situation you wish to happen, or in which you wish to be comfortable and enjoy yourself, but about which you currently have negative feelings, such as anxiety, guilt, anger, and so on.

While alone, write out in full detail and in the present tense (as though it is actually happening now) an elaborate account of what for you would be an *absolutely perfect* lovemaking encounter with your (or a cared for) partner. Start the account from the very earliest stages (i.e., thoughts and feelings about what might happen).

As you write this imaginary sequence out, heavily emphasize your pleasurable emotional and physical feelings. Describe the stimulation of all your five senses (touch, vision, hearing, taste, and smell). Write the imagery from your own point of view, for example, use descriptions such as "I am feeling very aroused as he gently strokes my hair. . . ."

In many ways this description will be similar to that used in the technique of "elaborated writing" (session 9), except that it refers to an hypothetical, future, absolutely perfect lovemaking encounter.

The desired length is such that it will take you a minimum of 10 minutes to read it aloud slowly. Put most of this time into any particular aspects of the lovemaking sequence that you would find difficult to handle. This is extremely important!

When you have finally completed your written imagery, read it aloud slowly, and tape record it. Then, in private, repeatedly listen to the tape. As you listen, do your best to pretend that what you are hearing is quite literally actually happening now! Try to make it as vivid and realistic in your imagination as possible. Allow yourself to experience whatever emotions emerge, be they positive and pleasurable or otherwise. Over and above imagining the sequence, "act out" any parts that lend themselves to this. For example, if the tape is saying: ". . . my breathing is getting faster and deeper, and my head is rolling from side to side in ecstasy . . . ," then don't just imagine these things happening, but actually make yourself breathe faster and deeper and roll your head from side to side! Of course, initially you will feel a complete fool actually making these movements, but do them anyway. The more awkward you feel acting out the script, the greater you need to do it, and the more benefit you will ultimately get from it!

Immediately after you have listened to the tape, on every occasion it is very useful to answer the following questions thoughtfully. Writing down your answers is usually most helpful. The aim is to make you really think about what is going on inside your mind!

1. Did I have any difficulty imagining any part of the imagery? If so, why?
2. Was it difficult to act out any part of the imagery? If so, why?
3. Did any parts of the imagery make me in any way "uptight"? If so, why?
4. Did any part or parts of the imagery appeal to me? If so, why?
5. Did any part of the imagery make me in any way sexually aroused? Is so, how did I know that I was sexually aroused?

When you feel that you can not only listen to and imagine, but also act out the script without any embarrassment or uptight feelings, see if you can listen to it with your partner. Of course, should you do this when he or she is present, do *not* act out the script! Repeat this shared listening until you feel totally comfortable with it.

When you feel you have thoroughly mastered this technique and feel quite comfortable with your own imagery, ask your partner to write out a sequence describing his or her ideal sexual encounter with you in the same detail but written from his or her point of view. Get your partner to make a tape recording of this, and then you practice it as before, alone. Remember, it is only an imaginary exercise, so allow yourself to fantasize whatever is described, even if it is something you have no wish to try. When you are quite comfortable doing this by yourself, repeatedly listen to it with your partner, as above.

Though a little time-consuming, this is an extremely useful technique in helping you to become aware of your innate sexual interest and overcome any negative emotions causing problems.

Session 14

Individual Stimulation Exercises

This is one of the most important exercises you can do to help yourself.

The plot is essentially this: In private, under good general conditions, manually fondle your lubricated genitals and master the various associated skills. Note that you are not trying to achieve orgasm—this is unwanted, unhelpful, and in fact forbidden.

Some General Rules for Doing These Exercises

1. You need good conditions. You must have guaranteed privacy and freedom from interruption, and your "conditions" for being responsive (chapter 7) must be met. If you have difficulty obtaining good circumstances under which to practice, your first task will be to rearrange your daily/weekly schedule so that you can. When there is a real will to succeed, you will find a way around problems, whatever the difficulties.

2. You must get into a sensual frame of mind first! There is no point trying these exercises immediately after you finish some unrelated chore. You might, for example, listen to your favorite music for a while, read or look at erotic material for a time, or perhaps enjoy a relaxed bath.

3. During the exercises, you *must concentrate on the physical sensations you are experiencing!* If necessary, use thought stopping to get rid of thoughts about anything else. In those exercises where you are required also to fantasize, you must still try to concentrate on your genital feelings. This takes a bit of practice, but it can be done! It may help to pretend that the feelings you are actually experiencing in your genitals are being produced by whatever is happening in the fantasy.

4. Strictly avoid *trying* to make anything happen. Remember, if you try to make yourself become aroused, you will make your problem worse, not better!

5. Make haste slowly! Do not move from one step to the next until you are *absolutely* sure you have mastered the goals of the present step. The commonest error is trying to go too fast.

6. In all the steps, do *not* begin touching youself on your genitals as soon as you start the exercise! First, "warm up" by pleasurably stroking other parts of your body, focusing on what you then feel. Make sure you are *completely relaxed* before you begin the genital touching part of the exercises. If necessary, use one of the formal quick relaxation methods described in session 6.

7. You must not ejaculate or have an orgasm during or after these exercises, unless it genuinely happens accidentally.

Step 1

In the first step, you explore and stimulate your genitals, focusing on your feelings, but without allowing even the slightest trace of arousal.

Use a suitable lubricant such as warmed-up baby oil. Close your eyes as you explore and manipulate yourself, and focus on what you are feeling. Immediately cease genital stimulation if you become aware of any trace of arousal. If you have to do this, continue pleasuring some other portion of your body until you are not aware of any trace of arousal. Then resume genital stimulation. Make sure you try different kinds of touching and stimulation—everything you can think of, although not necessarily in each and every session. Continue for approximately 15 minutes. If at the end of this time you feel that you would like to continue pleasuring yourself until you ejaculate or reach orgasm, *do not do so!* It is very important that you do *not* have an orgasm at the end of this exercise.

Repeat this first step on as many separate occasions as it takes for you to know that you have explored every kind of touching and stimulation you can think of on each and every portion of your genital area while focusing on your sensations. No matter what, *never* move to the next step until this first one has been practiced on at least six separate occasions. Usually you will need more practice than this!

Possible problems. The main one is that you feel just too emotionally uncomfortable about touching yourself to do these exercises at all. If this applies to you, use "desensitization" (appendix 8) to overcome these negative feelings. Remember also what I call the "gun at the head" analogy! It goes like this:

If I put a gun to the head of your dearest friend and said, "I will kill your friend if you don't do this self-stimulation exercise right now," then, of course, you would be able to make yourself do it! In other words, it's not that you can't do it, you merely find it difficult to do, or just don't want to do it. Don't make the mistake then of deceiving yourself that you can't do it. You *can* and you *must* if you are to succeed! Even if you have to *force* yourself and initially feel pretty uptight about it, with repeated practice it will get progressively easier. You owe it to yourself to at least try.

Step 2

In this step, you stimulate your genitals, focusing on your feelings until a degree of arousal has been achieved.

This is done exactly as in step 1, but now you will use the kinds of genital manipulation that you have learned are most stimulating. Don't forget the nongenital warm-up. Do not, under any circumstances, actively try to make yourself aroused. Simply stimulate yourself, focus on your genital feelings, and keep all other thoughts out of your mind, using thought stopping if necessary. Allow your body to do whatever it wants to do. As soon as you become aware of a little arousal, *immediately* stop genital stimulation and continue stroking and caressing your inner thighs and lower abdomen. When your arousal has completely gone, begin genital stimulation until you are again aware of a little arousal, then change over to nongenital caressing until it subsides completely. Continue thus for 20 minutes, then stop *without* giving yourself an orgasm at the end. This prohibition is *crucially* important.

When you repeat this exercise in the next practice session, continue stimulating yourself until you are just a little more aroused than you allowed yourself to become in the last exercise session.

When you repeat this exercise in your next practice period, continue until you are aroused just a little more than you permitted yourself in the previous session. Continue slowly progressing. After perhaps a dozen separate practice periods, you will be continuing stimulation until you are quite obviously aroused, both physically and mentally. Should you get any sensation that ejaculation or orgasm is not far away, *immediately* cease genital stimulation and do not resume it until any such feeling has completely and absolutely vanished. If you genuinely inadvertently ejaculate or reach orgasm, it can't be helped, so simply terminate the exercise for that occasion.

Remember:

1. Follow the instructions *exactly* as I have spelled them out.
2. Always get into the correct frame of mind first, and make sure you are completely relaxed and remain that way. Use a nongenital warm-up.
3. At all times, focus on your physical genital sensations.

4. Always lubricate your genitals, lower abdomen, and inner thighs.

5. Never try to become aroused—let your body do whatever it fancies on any particular occasion.

6. With repeated practice in different sessions, allow your arousal to increase only just a little more than you permitted in the previous session.

7. No orgasm!

8. Make haste slowly! If you finish this exercise in fewer than a dozen separate sessions, you are going too fast. Often many more than 12 sessions are required to properly master this sequence!

Possible problems. The main one is that your body might be behaving stubbornly, refusing to release arousal. If this occurs, check to make sure you have obeyed all my rules and instructions to the letter. If you haven't, get your conditions right and start all over again from the beginning, now doing this procedure exactly correctly. If you have in fact done it absolutely correctly, cut your losses and stop the exercise for this occasion. If you notice no arousal at all after several more sessions, simply skip this second step and move on to step 3.

How will you know that you are experiencing sexual arousal in this exercise? You might notice a vaguely pleasant, mild tingling sensation in your genitals. Men will usually observe some degree of expansion of their penis. Women may be aware of some vaginal lubrication. You might also notice a vaguely pleasant, mental or psychological feeling, which is impossible to describe but easy to recognize if you have had previous experiences in which you became sexually aroused.

Step 3

In this step, you stimulate your genitals, focusing on your feelings and a sexual fantasy, but without permitting sexual arousal.

This is done similarly to step 1 (self-stimulation, focusing on feelings, but without allowing even the slightest trace of arousal), except that now as you manipulate yourself you are to imagine one of the sexual fantasies you have been practicing (session 12). Remember, it takes some considerable practice to self-stimulate, focus on feelings, and lose yourself in a fantasy. Simply do your best, and in a dozen 15-minute practice sessions or so, you will have the hang of it. Continue practicing until you are fully confident that you can easily do it. If during step 3 you become aware of any arousal, continue with the fantasy but change to caressing and stimulating other skin areas nearby until it has completely disappeared.

Step 4

In this last step, you stimulate your genitals, focusing on your feelings and a sexual fantasy, permitting gradually increasing arousal.

This is done exactly as in step 2, but now you will use one of your favorite rehearsed sexual fantasies as well. In the first session, you will stop genital stimulation as soon as you get a tiny degree of arousal. In the second session, you will continue until it has increased just a little more. After many separate sessions, you continue until you are quite obviously aroused.

Deal with any feelings of impending ejaculation or orgasm as described in step 2.

Do not move on to the shared stimulation exercises until in this last step you are fully confident of your ability to become aroused without in any way trying to do so. Make haste slowly. Curb your impatience!

Even when you have fully mastered this step, continue practicing it by yourself, at least twice a week, until you have completely finished your self-help program.

Should your body *persistently* fail to cooperate by not permitting arousal despite your doing everything exactly as described and under good conditions, simply cut your losses and cease doing this exercise. Don't then worry or consider yourself a failure! Remember, not every exercise is right or helpful for every person. Progress then to the initial shared stimulation exercises.

What do you do if you haven't got a cooperative partner, and despite correctly performing this self-stimulation exercise, you still can't experience any degree of arousal at all?

This is the point at which you should seek professional assistance. You would first get your doctor meticulously to check you out for, and deal with, any physical contributions to your problem. Unless that fixes it, you would then seek expert sex therapy.

Session 15

Sexual Vocabulary Exercise

When talking about sex, sexual organs, and sexual behavior, it is much easier and more natural to use your own personal sexual vocabulary—something both you and your partner feel comfortable with.

Most people are put off by the use of technical terms such as penis, vulva, intercourse, etc. when talking to their partners. However, many couples have never actually negotiated with each other exactly what "pet" terms are and are not mutually acceptable.

In private, write down all the nontechnical words you can think of that describe the following scientific terms and that appeal to or are acceptable to you. Get your partner to do the same thing, also in private. Then together go through your lists and negotiate a final list of mutually acceptable terms. If you don't know a pet term, make one up!

The main technical words or phrases that are relevant are breasts, nipples, female genitals (vulva), clitoris, vagina, penis, testicles, being sexually interested, getting lubricated during arousal (female), an erection, oral sex (male on female (cunnilingus)), oral sex (female on male (fellatio)), being sexually aroused, female sexual secretions, reaching orgasm, seminal fluid, ejaculating, masturbation, hand stimulation of your partner's genitals to produce orgasm, intercourse, having intercourse, intercourse (male on top), intercourse (female on top), intercourse (rear entry), intercourse (both sitting facing each other), intercourse (female back against male front).

Write down your final list and deliberately use these words whenever you get a chance in appropriate circumstances. Don't worry if you feel a bit awkward or stupid to start off with—you will soon become perfectly comfortable.

Session 16

Sexual Communication Exercise

To do this, you will need to buy a suitable book on lovemaking. There are many excellent ones on the subject, available from all major booksellers. Purchase one that seems right for you after browsing through the whole range. Some are a bit highbrow, or hard to read, or boring. Others may be unsuitable for you for some particular reason. Many find Alex Comfort's *Joy of Sex* excellent, although it assumes that the reader starts off with a fair degree of sexual knowledge and sophistication. Theresa Crenshaw's *Your Guide to Better Sex* is excellent on attitudes, feelings, communication, and a variety of problems.

The book you choose is not being purchased to provide you with factual information, although virtually every couple practicing this exercise learns something new from whatever one they select. Its *primary use* is to help you and your partner learn to communicate easily and comfortably about all aspects of normal lovemaking and sexual expression. Here is how you use your book:

1. Read the first page aloud to your partner. As you do so, either of you are free to interrupt to comment and ask a question. At the end of the page, together discuss what has been read. When this has been done, your partner will read the next page to you in the same way.

2. Put a time limit of 15 minutes on this exercise, which, if possible, should be repeated every day. A little done often is far more rewarding than infrequent, lengthy sessions.

You will find that as you work through the book, it becomes easier and easier to express your own views and feelings about all the various aspects of lovemaking in a way that would not have been possible if you had merely discussed lovemaking together without the use of the book. Almost everyone who perseveres with this exercise, which may take many months to complete, reports that they have achieved the following:

1. A much greater awareness of their own individual sexuality, likes, dislikes, preferences, anxieties, fantasies.
2. A greatly increased awareness of their partner's sexuality, needs, wishes, dislikes, and preferences.
3. An ability easily and comfortably to discuss absolutely any aspect of sexual expression without shyness or embarrassment.

I think you will find that these benefits will greatly enhance your love-life together, indirectly decrease concerns about performance, and increase arousability and the effectiveness of sexual technique.

Session 17

Shared Sensuality Exercises

Let it be clearly stated at the outset that this exercise sequence is probably the most important single thing you and your partner can do together to resurrect your sex life! How well or otherwise you do this will determine more than anything else the ultimate quality of the sexual relationship you achieve together.

Do yourself a favor—perform these exercises thoroughly, and *strictly* according to the instructions, until you have clearly achieved all the specific goals.

Step 1

This is a touching exercise done naked. You must have good conditions for doing it: privacy, freedom from interruption, a warm room. Additionally, you must not be tired, uptight, or preoccupied. If you have difficulty finding half an hour under such conditions, there must be something wrong with your style of living, and your first task together will be to work out how you can get your circumstances right! The most common problem is getting privacy and having peace of mind when there are young children awake in the house. You may have to farm them out to a friend or relative for a few hours. If you are really motivated to overcome your problem, you will somehow find a way. Remember to take your phone off the hook!

Undress each other until you are totally naked. Then flip a coin or use some other democratic way to decide who will be the toucher to start with. The partner to be touched lies naked on the bed, face up or face down. The room light should be on. The toucher has the job of pleasurably touching the partner absolutely anywhere, but not on the breasts or genitals, which are strictly off-limits. The toucher is *not* in any way trying to arouse the partner sexually—the aim is just to produce nice feelings. Getting aroused is undesirable, unwanted, and a nuisance. Don't let it happen. Should one or other of you actually get turned on, that is just bad luck, as under no circumstances is this exercise to be followed by any form of sexual activity, including private masturbation. You will just have to try a long cold shower or a few hundred pushups, etc. to get rid of your arousal.

Don't make the mistake of touching your partner only with your hands. You can touch with your nose, lips, tongue, elbow, rump, big toe, and so on, and in due course you should try touching with all these and anything else you can think of. One of the ultimate goals is to have tried every conceivable kind of touching on every part of each other's body.

The person on the receiving end has the job of closing the eyes and giving a nonstop (literally that—without a pause) running commentary on what the touching feels like (in detail) and in what ways it is liked or disliked.

The touched person is at liberty to give specific directions, make requests, and so on.

After about 15 minutes you swap places so that the first toucher becomes the touched. Finish the exercise after about 15 minutes each way. If you don't feel like going for the full time on any particular occasion, stop sooner—for heaven's sake *don't force yourself* to stick it out for the recommended 15 minutes.

A possible problem. If you haven't had any sexual contact with your partner for a while, the idea of suddenly being naked together with the light on may be a bit embarrassing or even scary. You need to know that most couples actually feel a bit stupid or embarrassed the first time, perhaps because the whole performance is contrived and novel rather than spontaneous and familiar. It is perfectly all right to start off in a rather less embarrassing way if you feel like it! You might, for example, do it initially in the dark, or with night attire or underwear on, gradually progressing to complete nakedness with the light on.

Some variations. You may be interested in doing the exercise when the room is illuminated by a red light, or by candles. You will probably find that your bodies then look more sensual, and you may feel more comfortable when the worst of what ageing has done to you is rather less conspicuous!

In at least several sessions you should try the exercise with the aid of some body lotion or massage oil—you will find this a different, very sensual experience. If you are worried about messing up your sheets, use a couple of colored towels underneath you.

Particularly if you find yourselves a little light on ideas about different kinds of sensual, nonsexual touching, you might care to systematically work through the suggestions in a book on sensual massage. See the reading list in appendix 4.

Goals to be achieved before you move on to the second step:

1. You should have tried every kind of touching you can think of on every part of each other's body, except for the breasts and genitals.
2. You should feel *completely* relaxed during the exercise and actually enjoy the experience.
3. You should have mastered the art of nonstop talking about what you are feeling and how you like it or dislike it.
4. You should be very comfortable giving each other instructions as to exactly what you would like done to you.

I have never met any couple who have genuinely achieved these goals in fewer than six half-hour sessions, and I can tell you from considerable experience that most couples require many more than these six sessions to achieve their goals. Make haste slowly—these particular exercises are crucially important.

You may think all this sounds very simple (and it is!) and wonder how it could be so important. Suffice to say that in this apparently simple exercise there are actually a large number of important things happening which are not obvious at first.

It is a sad fact that for many people doing this exercise is the first opportunity they have had in their whole life to relate physically naked without any need to perform or achieve some particular goal!

Step 2

When you can honestly say that you have achieved all the goals of the first part of these exercises, you are ready for the next step. This is essentially the same as the first one, except that the focus of attention is exclusively on the breasts (both male and female) and genitals, for example, the parts of the body that were forbidden in the first exercise.

Even though sexual parts of your bodies are now going to be touched, you are not meant to get turned on or aroused! Getting aroused is actually a nuisance because it distracts you from really learning as much as you can about yourself and your partner. If you do become aroused, that is just bad luck, as there is no lovemaking or masturbation at the end! Try the cold shower treatment or something similar!

When exploring and fondling the female genital area, you simply *must* use some form of lubricant or you will cause discomfort. If you don't have a pleasantly perfumed body lotion or massage oil, you can use warmed-up baby oil.

Because the breast and genital areas are relatively small, many people make the mistake of thinking that it won't take long to fully explore them. Small they may be, but you need to examine them in meticulous detail! You might, for example, be seeing what one index finger rubbing gently on one square centimeter of one inner lip feels like. You aim to systematically explore the sensate (feeling) potential of every little nook and cranny, every area of skin. It will take you at least six half-hour sessions, and probably many more, to achieve the goals of step 2, which are the same as the goals of step 1.

Remember, under no circumstances are you to engage in any form of sexual activity, including masturbation, after either step of this exercise! You ignore this advice at your own peril.

Session 18

Exercises To Develop Trust and Emotional Closeness

For most people, a reasonable degree of trust in their partner is a prerequisite for satisfactory sexual relating. Lack of trust in your partner can be due to something he or she has actually done (or failed to do) in the past, or it can be due to you irrationally attaching to him or her an attitude of mistrust that developed from other sources in the past, perhaps before you even knew him or her.

Intimacy is a difficult-to-describe special emotional closeness with your partner in which you can be yourself as you feel at any moment without having to pretend, and where you are confident of your partner's unconditional caring and acceptance of you as a person, even if he or she disapproves of some of your behavior. Obviously, trust is a prerequisite for real intimacy. Whether we are consciously aware of it, we all crave intimacy. Sadly, however, many people are frightened of it and start to backpedal when they begin to get emotionally close. *Ideally,* sexual relating is an exercise in intimacy, and for well-mated couples that very special feeling of closeness becomes the most important and fulfilling aspect of lovemaking, transcending and surpassing much less relevant issues such as arousal, intercourse, and orgasm.

The *only* way to develop trust and intimacy is to have experiences which promote and teach these qualities. They are *not* in any way necessarily an automatic consequence of being in love. Sometimes, unfortunate past experiences have to be laid to rest before trust and intimacy can be allowed to develop.

Promoting Trust and Intimacy

1. Your partner can try to be as helpful and supportive as possible, avoid any pressure over sex, and listen to and respect your points of view (even though he or she may disagree with them). You can reciprocate generously and in kind.

2. While having a nonsexual cuddle in private (if that is possible), talk together about the level of trust between you. If it is not as high as you would wish, discuss what you can both do to increase it. When you do this, bend over backwards not to be seen as critical or condemnatory, as this will usually put your partner on the defensive and may lead to bad feelings or even an argument. Try ways of presenting your views for what they really are, for example, just your point of view! You might say, "It seems to me, rightly or wrongly . . . ," or, "I'm probably being totally unreasonable, but . . . ." Try to negotiate a mutually acceptable plan for improving things, rather than present to your partner a series of "you musts."

3. Work out a "physical trust position." Talk about and experiment to develop one or two positions involving physical contact that you find "safe", where you feel a combination of closeness and trust. Try lying on your sides, simply holding each other with as much body contact as possible. Try one of you sitting up, comfortably supported, cradling the other's head in your lap, stroking his or her hair. Try lying next to each other, simply holding hands. Try the "spoons" position—your back against his or her stomach with you curled up on yourself.

Experiment also to find out what adds to your sense of trust and closeness: the presence or absence of different types of body contact, eye contact, being enveloped, talking, stroking, and so on. When you have worked out your ideal trust position or positions, use it (them) as often as possible when you have some time together. Use it also during lovemaking should you in any way begin to feel "uptight." It won't instantly fix everything, but it will help you to feel better and more trusting.

4. You may have to "lay the past to rest" so that past happenings don't affect the way you feel and behave in the present. You might use "elaborate writing" (session 9), "desensitization" (session 8), or one of the "talking sense to yourself" techniques (session 3) to achieve this end.

5. You might have to really work hard to overcome the effects of one or several particularly damaging sexual myths resisting change. See chapter 6 and session 4.

6. You might have to work to change some unhelpful general attitudes contributing to your trust/intimacy problem, using one of the books on attitude change listed in appendix 4.

If you sit down and think about it, you will discover that nearly all the joint exercises I have suggested will, amongst other things, promote trust and greater closeness. Reflect on how this might result from the following:

Sexual vocabulary exercise (session 15)
Sexual communication exercise (session 16)
Sharing sexual fantasies (session 12)
Shared sensuality exercises (session 17)
Listening to your partner's guided imagery tape (session 13)
Shared stimulation exercises (session 19)

Should you realize that lack of trust is a significant factor contributing to your sexual drive deficiency, you must appreciate that it will take some considerable time (at least many months) to establish a reasonable degree of trust. Don't let yourself or your partner become discouraged over this slow process. If you quietly keep trying, you will get there in the end, and then value even more greatly what you have achieved together.

Session 19

Shared Stimulation Exercises

Before you start these, you must have thoroughly worked through the individual stimulation exercises described in session 14 and the shared sensuality exercises as described in session 17.

Before you go any further, reread session 14, as you will now be doing something very similar together.

Note carefully the general rules!

Position for this exercise. Most couples find the best positions to be as follows:

For women, the position depicted in figure 1. Your male partner, who is naked, sits upright in bed with his back supported by pillows placed against the bed-head or wall. His legs are reasonably straight and fairly wide apart. You sit naked with your back against his chest, facing away from him. Your legs are wide apart and lie over his. Your buttocks are on the bed, or if more comfortable, on a small cushion.

For men, the position depicted in figure 2. Your female partner, who is naked, sits upright in bed with her back supported by pillows placed against the bed-head or wall. Her legs are reasonably straight and fairly wide apart. You lie naked on your back in the opposite direction, your head facing the other end of the bed. Your legs are over her thighs so that your genital area is quite comfortably within her reach, close to her own genitals.

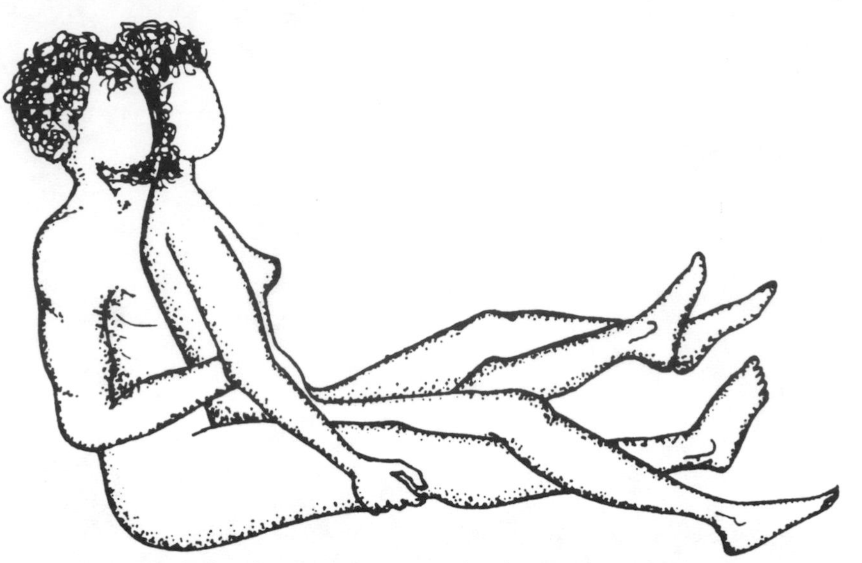

Fig. 1. The preferred position for women for the shared stimulation exercise.

Making love after this exercise. Sometimes after performing this exercise you will feel like making love. This is perfectly okay, so long as the exercise and your spontaneous lovemaking are clearly separated in both your minds. If your partner isn't actively in the mood for lovemaking or feels anti-it, follow the suggestions covering these situations described in chapter 10.

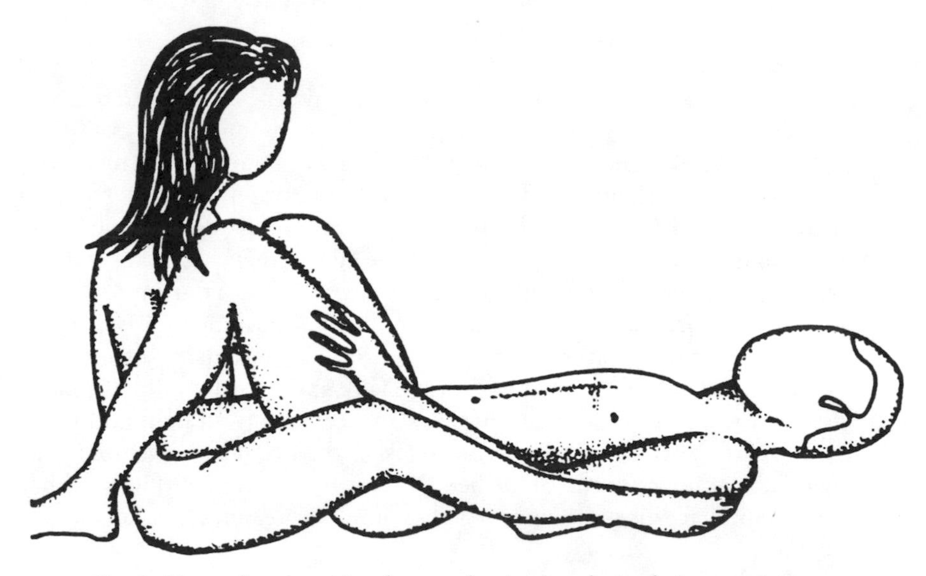

Fig. 2. The preferred position for men for the shared stimulation exercise.

Step 1

First your partner stimulates your genitals, while you focus on your feelings, but without allowing even the slightest trace of arousal.

The instructions are generally as for session 14, step 1, except that your partner is now providing the stimulation. Because you have already done the shared sensuality exercises together, your partner is *not* required to explore your genitals as you did by yourself.

After at least six practice sessions, and then only when you are totally confident that in this exercise you can easily focus on your physical genital sensations and remain completely relaxed, move onto the next step.

Step 2

In the second step, your partner stimulates your genitals, while you focus on your feelings, until a degree of arousal has been achieved.

The directions are essentially the same as in step 2, session 14, but with your partner providing the stimulation. Together reread the instructions there very carefully. Remember, under no circumstances are you to try to get aroused! Let your body do whatever it chooses on any particular occasion.

Continue this step in repeated sessions until you are totally confident that in this exercise you can easily and consistently become quite obviously aroused both physically and mentally.

Step 3

In this step, your partner stimulates your genitals, without any arousal permitted, while you use a sexual fantasy and continue to focus on your genital feelings.

This is done similarly to step 1 above, except that now as you are stimulated you are to imagine one of the sexual fantasies you have been practicing (session 12). Remember, it takes some considerable practice to focus on feelings and lose yourself in a fantasy while you are being stimulated.

Do this exercise for about 15 minutes and repeat it as many times as necessary until you are fully confident that you can easily do it.

If during this step you become aware that you are getting aroused, continue with the fantasy, but get your partner to caress and stimulate other skin areas nearby until you are no longer aroused.

Step 4

In this last step, your partner stimulates your genitals, while you use a sexual fantasy and focus on genital feelings with progressively increasing arousal permitted.

See step 4, session 14, but continue for about 30 minutes. Note that ejaculation or orgasm is to be avoided during this exercise unless it genuinely happens inadvertently. Repeat this step until, after as many separate sessions as it takes, you are consistently and easily quite obviously aroused both physically and mentally.

A note for partners. It is clearly acknowledged that there is nothing much for you in these exercises! They represent something that you are doing to help your partner, because you care and want to assist. However, you will be *well rewarded* in the long run!

Appendixes

Appendix 1

Overcoming Associated Sexual Dysfunctions

For the female, this most often will be a difficulty in reaching orgasm, or an inability to do so. This common problem usually responds to self-help measures under guidance, and I would recommend the program described in the book *Becoming Orgasmic* (see appendix 4).

For men, the most common difficulties will be erectile problems and premature ejaculation. If you have difficulty obtaining or maintaining an adequate erection, you might read my book *It's Up to You* (see appendix 4), which describes in full detail the relevant issues and how you can help yourself. If you cannot delay your ejaculation and usually climax sooner than you would wish, you could follow the self-help program described in *Men and Sex* (see appendix 4).

It goes without saying that there are limitations on what can be achieved by self-help procedures, and if you find yourself not benefiting from these programs, you should seek referral to an appropriately trained therapist.

Should you have other sexual problems not described here, it would probably be best, at least in the first instance, to consult with a professional person who should be able to advise you of your most appropriate course of action.

Appendix 2

Some Sexual "Bad Habits" To Be Avoided or Overcome

Strictly speaking, some of these issues are largely beyond the immediate subject of this book, but I have chosen to include a brief section on bad habits. Why? First, some of what I have to say will be a useful revision of issues I have raised earlier. Second, having shown you how to revamp your sex life, I would hate to think that you ran the risk of getting less out of sexual relating than you could merely because I didn't remind you of a few simple facts.

The following bad habits are offered in no particular order and with minimal elaboration. A little thought should enable you to see what is wrong.

1. Ignoring your "conditions" for being sexually interested and responsive! This, of course, applies to both you and your partner, and for the pair of you will become progressively more important as you grow older.

2. Sameness! Do you always make love in basically the same way? Do you usually do it at approximately the same time, in the same place? Would you enjoy your favorite food if all you ate day in and day out was the same food at the same time, in the same place?

3. Always leaving lovemaking until bedtime! You can't expect to be creative, sensitive, intuitive, active, and sensuous when you are tired at the end of a long day.

4. Fondling breasts and genitals too quickly after starting, neglecting cuddling together, slow kissing, and caressing other parts of the body.

5. The male doing the inserting of the penis. It should *always* be the woman's job!

6. Failing to talk during lovemaking. You should be conveying endearments and, even more importantly, requests, information, and feedback about your wishes and needs.

7. Talking about unrelated events during lovemaking. Your partner gets a very clear message that your mind is elsewhere, which is a real slap-in-the-face for someone who is trying to express his or her love for you.

8. Being preoccupied with other issues during lovemaking! If you can't devote yourself mentally to what you are experiencing and sharing, what on earth are you doing making love? This is much more than simply bad manners—it is *stupidity* of a very hurtful kind, and frankly insulting to your partner!

9. Habitually not having enough time for proper lovemaking! Are you always or often making love, as it were, with one eye on a mental clock?

10. Putting pressure on your partner to have an orgasm. Lovemaking has nothing to do with performance or pressure! Orgasms are *not* in any way essential.

11. Wearing clothing that turns your partner off during lovemaking.

12. Making love when you are smelly!

13. Making love with unclean genitals!

14. Never having an orgasm other than inside the vagina, or for women, one produced by penile thrusting!

15. Never having a nonsexual break during lovemaking. If once you start sexual contact it *must* relentlessly proceed until intercourse has been achieved and finished, you are missing out on the joys of stop-start lovemaking! This does not mean that you should dive out of bed and mow the lawn between oral-genital stimulation and intercourse, but it does mean that sometimes after arousing each other to a degree, you might just talk, have a laugh, cuddle, enjoy some music, before again commencing sexual stimulation. Who wants to rush through a fabulous four-course meal without a break between dishes! Stop to enjoy the atmosphere and whet the appetite a little so that the experience can be as pleasurable as possible.

16. Ceasing all physical and verbal expressions of affection as soon as intercourse finishes. In old-fashioned language, *don't forget the "afterplay"!*

17. Always having the light off when you make love.

18. Hopping out of bed to wash your genitals immediately after intercourse. If you still think sex is dirty, you have a lot of growing up to do!

19. Only showing your partner affection when you want sexual contact.

20. Never engaging in pleasurable physical contact with your partner's sexual organs except when you intend to carry through and have intercourse. Playful, gentle, loving genital and breast stimulation should be part and parcel of daily affectionate body contact.

Isn't it easy to slip into some bad habits without really realizing that it is happening?

Appendix 3

Some Hints on the First Time With a New Partner

Most men and women feel at least some anxiety the first time they have sex with a new partner, unless perhaps it is a purely commercial transaction. The reasons for this are numerous, but in essence we tend to feel somewhat insecure in this situation, because we are then potentially so emotionally vulnerable. Of course, some people go to great lengths to try to conceal their anxiety, but the astute observer can still pick it up!

The Basic Rule

Never under any circumstances get into a sexual situation with a new partner unless most of your personal conditions for being sexually interested and responsive are met. Remember the message of chapter 7.

It is especially important that you *don't* get into a sexual encounter if you are in any way tense, anxious, angry, guilty, and so on.

Some Important Points

1. First, get to know your partner over a number of social meetings to get comfortable with him or her and to determine if you really want to have sex with him or her.

2. Remember, there is no law that says you have to have sex just because you have an opportunity to do so, or because you are with a partner who wants to. If you don't feel comfortable or don't feel like sex, you could say something like this: "It probably sounds quaint, but making love is something special to me, and as much as you turn me on, I choose to wait until I know you better. It will be much more enjoyable for both of us then." Far from causing your partner to think there is something wrong with you, he or she will respect you all the more for this approach.

3. You don't have to "go all the way" first up! You will probably find yourself feeling much more comfortable if you, as it were, wade in gradually, in stages. You could, for example, start with a simple massage for the first few times, then progress to deliberate breast and genital stroking and so on. You might perhaps say something like this: "I guess I'm old-fashioned, but intercourse is something really special for me, and I'd like to know you better in every way before we become completely intimate. We'll both enjoy it so much more then."

4. A neat, effective way of decreasing your anxiety is to *admit to being anxious.* Try to express it in a light-hearted manner, for example, by saying something like this: "It is totally ridiculous, since I feel extremely close to you and very much want to make love with you, but I feel a little anxious—isn't it stupid." By admitting it, you largely overcome it. Often enough, your partner will have a laugh and confess to being anxious also, in which case you can both relax, because there is no longer any need to pretend.

5. Remember what I have said about "leveling" in chapter 18.

Appendix 4

Recommended Reading

Sexual Myths, Conditions for Being Sexually Interested and Responsive, Dealing With Problems

Zilbergeld, Bernie. *Men and Sex.* Medindie, South Austria: Souvenir Press, 1978. (The American edition is titled *Male Sexuality,* and was published by Little, Brown & Company, Boston, 1978.)

Crenshaw, Theresa. *Your Guide to Better Sex.* Sidney: Rigby Publishers, 1985.

Attitude Change

Lazarus, Arnold, and Allen Fay. *I Can If I Want To.* New York: William Morrow and Company, 1975.

Ellis, Albert, and Robert Harper. *A New Guide to Rational Living.* Hollywood: Wilshire Book Company, 1975.

Shared Sensuality Exercises

Inkeles, Gordon, and Murray Todris. *The Art of Sensual Massage.* Wellington, New Zealand: Alister Taylor Publishing, 1973.

Sexual Fantasy

Friday, Nancy. *My Secret Garden.* New York: Trident Press, 1973.

______. *Forbidden Flowers.* New York: Pocket Books, 1975.

______. *Men in Love.* London: Hutchinson & Company, 1980.

(The first two are on female fantasies and the third is about male fantasies. All are worth reading by men and women!)

Lovemake Techniques

Comfort, Alex. *The Joy of Sex*. London: Quartet Books, 1985.

Specific Sexual Problems

Williams, Warwick. *It's Up to You—Self-help for Men With Erection Problems*. Sydney: Williams & Wilkins, Adis, 1985.

Heiman, Julia, Leslie LoPiccolo, and Joseph LoPiccolo. *Becoming Orgasmic: A Sexual Growth Program for Women*. New Jersey: Prentice-Hall, 1976.

You should be able to borrow these books from any sizeable library, even if it has to get them in for you. Alternatively, you could purchase them from any major bookseller, although they might have to be specially ordered for you.

Appendix 5

A Simple Description of Some Technical Terms Used in This Book

Amphetamine	A stimulant drug like caffeine, but more powerful.
Angina	Chest pain due to inadequate blood flow to the heart.
Antidepressant	A drug useful in overcoming a depressive illness.
Aphrodisiac	A drug stimulating sexual interest.
Autosuggestion	Giving oneself suggestions while in a relaxed state.
Aversion	Avoidance of physical contact that could lead to sex. Associated with an automatic negative emotional reaction to sex or the possibility of sex.
Caffeine	A stimulant drug found in coffee, tea, and cola beverages.
Chronic	Present for a long time.
Clitoris	A tiny, very sexually sensitive structure at the top of a woman's genitals. Female equivalent of the penis.
Cocaine	A stimulant drug with effects similar to amphetamine.

Compulsive	Obligatory, hard to resist.
Cunnilingus	Oral stimulation of the female genital organs.
Desensitization	A psychological treatment for inappropriate anxiety (or inappropriate guilt, anger, and so on).
Dysfunction	Malfunction.
Dysphoria	A general term for any unpleasant emotional state such as anger, anxiety, guilt, and so on.
Ejaculation	The expulsion of seminal fluid from the urinary passage to the exterior.
Fantasy (sexual)	A series of thoughts about a sexual subject, with or without associated mental pictures.
Fellatio	Oral stimulation of the penis.
Frigidity	A derogatory term for lack of sexual interest. Usually applied by men to women.
Genitals	The external sexual organs involved in reproduction.
Gustatory	To do with the sense of taste.
Hormone	A chemical produced by a gland in the body. Necessary for the normal functioning of some other body organ or organs.
Hypomania	An abnormal state of mental excitement. Not as severe as mania.
Incest	Sexual contact between family members.
Instinct	An innate drive or impulse present in us all.
Libido	Sexual drive or interest.
Limbic System	Part of the brain located around the rim or limbus. Concerned (amongst other functions) with sex.
Mania	An abnormal state of mental excitement. More severe than hypomania.
Masturbation	Fondling one's own genitals to produce pleasurable feelings and often (but not necessarily) orgasm.
Meditation	A group of techniques resulting in focusing of attention and relaxation.
Nymphomania	Excessive sexual drive in a woman.
Orgasm	The sudden, intensely pleasurable feeling that represents the height or climax of sexual arousal and enjoyment.
Pheromones	Chemicals secreted by humans and animals which can sexually attract members of the opposite sex through the sense of smell.
Phobia	An irrational fear of something leading to avoidance of it.

Premack Principle	A simple psychological procedure for making desired thoughts or behavior occur more frequently.
Prognosis	Outlook for cure or improvement.
Satyriasis	Excessive sexual desire in the male.
Secondary Gains	Fringe benefits of having an illness or disability, such as compensation, avoiding work, getting out of undesired sex, and so on.
Sedative	A drug that makes one calm and often drowsy.
Sensuality	Awareness of and pleasure in experiencing one or more of the body's senses (touch, hearing, vision, taste, and smell).
Testosterone	Male hormone.
Thought Stopping	A simple psychological procedure for getting unwanted thoughts out of one's mind.
Tranquilizer	A drug that calms without usually making one drowsy.
Unconscious Mind	That part of our mental processes of which we are not consciously aware.
Venereal Disease	A sexually transmitted disease.
Vibrator	An electrical gadget. When activated produces rapid back and forward movements of either the whole device or a portion of the device.
Vulva	The external sexual organs of a woman. Made up of inner and outer lips, and the clitoris.

HIEBERT LIBRARY
3 6877 00021 0764